I0140096

AMBITION
FACTOR

Rewriting the story of working mothers

ANA PAULA TEDIOSI

Published by Clink Street Publishing and Birdhaus Writing and Publishing 2021

Copyright ©2021

First edition.

The author asserts the moral rights under the Copyright, Design and Patent Act 1988 to be identified as the author of this book.

All rights reserved. No part of this publication maybe be reproduced, stored in a retrieval system or transmitted, in any form or by any means without the prior consent of the author, nor be otherwise circulated in any form of binding or cover other than that with which it is published and without a similar condition being imposed on the subsequent purchaser.

ISBN: paperback 978-1-913568-34-4
ISBN: ebook 978-1-913568-35-1

Dedicated to Riccardo,
of course.

Table of contents

Introduction

Do you remember the fairy tale Cinderella?

Of course, you do. It is about a beautiful girl who is the cleaning maid of her stepsisters and stepmother. Thanks to a little blue fairy, who by the way comes out of nowhere, she gets a beautiful dress, a fancy gig, goes to the ball in the castle, meets the prince, and has the time of her life. She needs to run back home at midnight because her elegant drive will transform into a pumpkin, and her dreamy outfit will disappear. But, fate steps in. She leaves behind a crystal shoe. The charming prince finds it and then saves her from her stepfamily, brings her back to the castle where she becomes a princess, and lives happily ever after.

In the current era of women's empowerment, this is a ridiculous story no girl should hear as a child. There is no such thing as a magical power that can save you from your misery. No one will never wear crystal shoes and dance the whole night away like Cinderella did. No man will marry you after one dance. But most important: no girl should sit, playing the victim of her circumstances, and wait for someone to save her and give her the happily ever after.

Let's transform this fairytale into a modern tale. A modern realistic retelling of Cinderella's story: there is a woman who is working for a challenging boss all day long. Her look is not very glamorous. Her last hairdresser appointment was one season ago. In her most recent shopping session for herself, she had five pounds less around her midsection. Her makeup routine is condensed into a five-minute hurried session.

Even the world around her is dull. When she walks in the door of her tiny one-bedroom apartment, the Bluetooth speaker that had been left on all day announces very little news of interest to her. Then one shining moment, the radio announcer mentions a glamourous party that is to be held at a billionaire's mansion. All proceeds go to charity. The Bluetooth speaker is immediately muted at this unwelcome reminder that she can't go to those types of things anymore.

She changes into more comfortable clothes and looks around with despair at the mess around the place she calls a living room. Her kids start to claim her attention as soon as they see her. Her husband is somewhere around the house doing whatever he fancies, while she cooks, takes care of the kids, and thinks about her family's schedule for the next day. When night comes, she goes to bed exhausted, trying to remember the last time she had fun or a workout session. She succumbs in a blissful sleep. Her life cruises like this for years, in a simple yet exhausting routine managing a day job plus housework plus kids, then repeat. One day, looking at her reflection in the mirror, she takes an inventory of her body and life, both shapeless in a twilight zone between happiness and despair. She realizes she is life-cruising in an existence that she does not really enjoy but does not hate. She waits for something to happen to bring her joy. She waits for her happily ever after that she had always dreamed of.

Ok, this is not so amusing. Both tales are hopeless for different reasons. Of course, you will never tell the second story to your children. How could you? What if we could find something real and gratifying within the chaos of a life full of work on repeat?

Let's try again.

Somewhere in the world, there is Valeria, a working mother who has a hectic but satisfying life. She has a good job, a lovely family, and she has plans for the future. She focuses on what matters most, works hard and continues to develop herself. Her look is not very glamourous, but her hair, clothing, and makeup are well kept. She could dedicate more time to her daily care. Her kids are the priority in the morning. She does her best to look put together and keep going.

When she comes back home from a day of work, the radio speaker in her kitchen sings with good news. It tells her that there will be sunny weather, perfect for outdoor activities with the family. Other good news: there are new companies opening close to her city, this means new opportunities. She needs to investigate more. More news: a big fancy party will take place in a club downtown. That, she will pass on, no time for dancing.

At home, she changes into more comfortable clothes. Her kids start to claim her attention as soon as she walks through the door. Her little beasts are the most important thing in her world. They will grow, eventually, and she will have her work to focus on. She feels energetic! Today was a good day. She was even able to carve out a part of her lunch break to go for a run!

Her partner helps her with the evening routine while discussing the weekly schedule and plans for the weekend. She is blessed with a lovely husband by her side. Even if he'll never remember to schedule the six-year old's checkup with the pediatrician, he is doing way more than the average partner would.

When night comes, she falls hard on her bed and drifts into a blissfully deep sleep. Some nights, when they are not too exhausted, a good round of sex reminds them that they are a couple with sexual needs. Yep, let's not forget that.

Her life is challenging and rewarding. Some days she feels it is too much and needs to find time for balance again. She is happy to be able to keep thriving both at work and with her family. She is looking forward to new opportunities that will inevitably open up for her and her family. She wants more, and that translates into better things for herself and her family.

Would this be a better story to tell a little girl? Is this less of a dream than Cinderella's story? And then what happens to Valeria? How has she kept her balance? How does she cultivate her ambitions in the middle of family responsibility? How did she share her responsibilities with her partner?

Most importantly, does she have moments of self-doubt where she thinks, "It is just too much" and wants to give up everything? Yes, of course, she does. Valeria is a snapshot of the modern ambitious working mother. And what if I tell you that Valeria was the woman of the first tale too? How did she shift from that to an energized and healthy woman full of drive and optimism?

This book is about real stories of working mothers who are defining their own "happily ever after" by following their ambitions. I want to share stories about women who are like you and me, who are trying their best to take care of their family while keeping their professional life on track and still have quality time for themselves. I want to discuss how some of us are coping with the challenges that working parents face every day and provide some tips on what we can implement to solve some challenges. And I want you to immerse yourself in Valeria's story and learn with her how to overcome them.

I would have liked to have this book around when work, family and life got to be too much. I would have read it during those moments when I felt like I'm failing at everything and I don't have the energy to keep going. It is during these times that I question my professional ambitions and my priorities in life. I question why I am working so hard. I wonder why all the efforts I'm putting in place are not leading to better job opportunities, equilibrate family life, and a healthy lifestyle?

Ambition is in all of us. We need it to fuel our daily routine, keep going forward, keep wanting more for our families, seek professional fulfillment, and reach gender equality at home and in the workplace. Observing ambitious women around me and in the world, I notice some patterns, similar elements here and there, which make the difference between working mothers cruising in their lives, and the ones who are thriving, because they embrace their **Ambition Factor**.

We don't have to be a celebrity, a famous CEO or the founder of a unicorn start-up to inspire other women to lead a fulfilled life by following their ambitions. After years of meeting them, networking with them and learning from them, I felt the urge to analyze and share which elements motivate women's ambitions and how working mothers keep thriving while coping with everything else. What started with the willingness to share how professionally active mothers are surfing the wave of life, became a desire to learn what ambition means nowadays.

Yes, we are ambitious working mothers. We are not the only ones. We are not alone.

We are not the only ones having the **Ambition Factor**, pushing us to want more out of our professional lives. We are not the only ones desiring a fulfilled and happy family life. We are not the only ones who need more time for ourselves. And we are not the only ones who want to surround ourselves with like-minded people who encourage and support us.

You are not alone in this. Read this book, embrace your ambition, build your tribe for support, shape a healthy and sustainable lifestyle, aim for more and better in all parts of your life.

I'm an Ambitious Woman, And You Are Too.

Valeria steps up onto the modern commuter train that takes her home every day at 4:30pm sharp. She walks briskly through the cramped corridors to her seat: F76. This was **her seat***. She crashed onto the chair, completely exhausted. She shoved her work bags to the ground below her, wishing that she could also strip herself of her work-home life frustrations. She was tired again. This is the* **mom tired,** *you know when you feel like your sugars are really low; like your mind is racing like a formula one car and like every inch of your body aches from exhaustion. Yeah, that tired.*

Valeria stared out the window of the train, watching it roll out of the station. She had thirty minutes to think peacefully about her chaotic and frustrating day at work, where she felt like she did absolutely nothing important or worth mentioning. **Is this really the life that I want?** *She asked herself, as she reflected over her missed opportunities that day. She had been late to work that day, had missed a very important marketing meeting and she had managed to pour a hot cup of coffee all over one of the board of directors' of her company. The other two events of the day had zapped all of her confidence, so she was not her best self during the last meeting* **Am I wasting all of these energies? Am I too tired to keep up?** *Ashamed and discouraged Valeria shook her head at herself.*

But she wasn't the type to wallow in her regrets. She needed to make a plan. **What can I do? Is there anyone that can help me?** *Valeria started to wonder if her frustrations were not a result of lack of energy but lack of focus.* **Do I know exactly what my life's ambition is? What exactly am I working for anyway? What is my purpose?** *Valeria suddenly felt the tension of her body release as she focused her mind on her desires, instead of her failure. The landscape that flashed by her suddenly looked more peaceful, slower even. It was in that moment that Valeria realized that she was more interested in the art and creativity of marketing, rather than the business of marketing. She wanted to express her artistic side. That is why she had wanted to connect with the head of Digital Design. She wanted to gain an understanding of how that department worked, imagining it to be much more exciting and rewarding than her current role. Having come to this realization, Valeria began to see her position differently. On that all too short train ride home, Valeria restructured her ambition towards what she knew that she really wanted.*

The Word Ambition

I love this word. Ambition.

Why is that? Because it triggers so many emotions, especially conflicting ones.

A couple of years ago, I wrote a blog post about the book *Career Advice for Ambitious Women* by Miss Money Penny, aka Heather McGregor[1]. This publication was my first interaction with self-development tools and the start of a fantastic self-discovery journey.

I define myself as an ambitious woman, of course. But what does it mean for me? When working in big companies, ambition usually means you want to climb the corporate ladder, become a manager, then a department director, then general manager, and continuing higher and higher. Strangely enough, it was never my definition of ambition nor my goal.

Some time ago, I did a profiling test from a well-known and established platform, and the results were a big surprise. This assessment told me that I need to show more drive, be more assertive, and prioritize my objectives more often in the workplace. In other words: I need to be more ambitious in my professional life.

I read the analysis with disbelief and humor and wondered if this was a mistake. If there is one thing I know about myself, I'm an ambitious person, and I don't lack personal drive.

Recalling the questions, however, I suspected why the result was like this. My inner drive was assessed by my intention to achieve top positions, the way I would behave during a business meeting, and my life priorities.

Do I want to become the CEO of a big pharmaceutical company? No!
Do I push my team to achieve an objective at any cost? No!
Am I ready to sacrifice my personal life to get the 'job of my dreams'? No!

Still, I challenge anyone who knows me to say I'm not an ambitious person. I am proud of my list of distinguished positions: a successful pharmaceutical career, small-business owner, author and blogger, working mother, and leader of a female nonprofit organization for five years. I work restlessly to achieve my objectives while keeping an open mind and listening to all suggestions around me, and I put my personal life and health as a priority.

The real question is: what does ambition mean? Is ambition only about a hefty paycheck and a fancy role in the company? How do you assess your aspiration in the era of working for a purpose? How do you find your WHY, while also cultivating a healthy and sustainable lifestyle? What if we need to change our way of assessing our inner drives?

These questions kept coming into my head for several days, and I decided I needed to dig deeper.

What the Literature Says

The Cambridge Dictionary defines 'ambition' as: *"a strong wish to achieve something; a strong wish to be successful, powerful, rich, etc."*[2]

There are plenty of articles, studies, and books around this topic mostly focused on the American population and culture. A book that I would recommend on the subject is *The Ambition Decisions: What Women Know About Work, Family, and the Path to Building a Life*, written by Hana Schank and Elizabeth Wallace[3]. The book follows the journey of Schank and Wallace, two American journalists who were both challenged by career and family upheaval in their forties. They decided to contact their sorority sisters from back in their days at Northwestern University in Chicago. What started with simple calls transformed into in-depth and personal interviews, research, a series of articles, and ultimately their book.

The publication describes the reflections and findings of women who were very ambitious in their twenties. These women decided to join a prestigious university and had big dreams and clear career objectives. The book's revealing findings are many, and I often wondered what results would come if a similar study was conducted in Swiss universities. One of the most significant findings as part of their research was that up until the point of the birth of the woman's first child, women had very similar objective trajectories: 1) Reach a specific level within her career; 2) Achieve financial security; 3) Build a family (the study interestingly noted that not all of the women interviewed wanted children). After the birth of the first child, their lives diverged within three groups:

· **The High Achievers** (full-time job and very committed to their career or business)
· **Flex-Lifers** (part-time worker, business owner or career in companies)
· **Opt-Outers** (The mothers who decided to stay home with their children)

The women in all categories, in a way or another, retain their ambition. The Opt-Outers, who left behind their career or business objectives to focus on caring for their family, channeled their ambition into their home, volunteer work and self-care. Some of the Flex-Lifers decided to slow down their careers while the kids were small and only to rev it back up when their families were less needy. A crucial aspect coming from Schank and Wallace's interviews was the fluidity of life trajectories. Women who decided to Opt-

Out turned into high achievers later in life. The same shift was noted in the High-Achievers, who chose to stop their careers and completely change their lives (Schank & Wallace, 2018).

"[In the past] one rarely moved from being a housewife to being an executive, and obviously, the option to work part-time from home was very limited. Our generation, by contrast, inherited not only the potential to be kicked-ass working women, but also something equally valuable: the luxury to reshape our work lives. Our friends have realized over the course of their lives that their careers path don't have to mirror their mothers. They have more choices and flexibility than their mother did and accordingly, they have been High Achievers, Opt Outer, and Flex Lifers all in one career lifetime."[4]

Christina Vuleta, a former editor at Forbes Women, referenced a study conducted by a global talent consulting company that aimed to measure women's professional aspirations and how age and country impacted their ambitions[5]. The fundamental question driving the research was, *"Why do women feel nervous and almost guilty about admitting to having ambitions, but men don't?"* The outcome showed that while young professional women aspire to reach executive ranks, ambition gaps emerge later in the career. Their country's economic development played an important role in their drive to succeed. *"More women in developing countries aspire to be in the senior ranks than in developed countries."*

Anna Fels, a psychiatrist and a faculty member at Cornell University's Weill Medical College in New York, conducted her research in the early 2000s publishing her results in 2004[6]. The answer to the question, *"Is there an ambition gap between genders?"* came with the understanding that ambition has two components: [7]
A. The mastery of some specific skills and
B. The recognition of that mastery by others

"In nearly all of the childhood ambitions, two undisguised elements were joined together. One was mastery of a special skill: writing, dancing, acting, diplomacy. The other was recognition: attention from an appreciative audience. Looking through studies on the development of both boys and girls, I noticed that they virtually always identified the same two components of childhood ambition. There was a plan that involved a real accomplishment requiring work and skill, and there was an expectation of approval in the form of fame, status, acclaim, praise, or honor. [...] This, for women, is why early aspirations so often do not translate into achievement later in life: A lack of appropriate affirmation of accomplishments in combination with threats to women's sexual identity inevitably leads to demoralization." [8]

When women and men re-evaluate their life's ambition, often women are more likely to downscale their goals because the effort that it takes to achieve their goals and ambitions is not as rewarded or endorsed by the broader society. Fels digs into the past and analyzes the evolution of women's part in society, linking women's professional and social achievements with losing her feminine role.

"[Women] are labeled as bluestockings or spinsters or agamic (the Victorian term for women who pursued higher education and were therefore considered asexual). In the present, this painful questioning occurs when career women move beyond the student or early career stage and are trying to start families. Many articles and books caution that career women will fail to get married, or, if they do get married, will be unable to have children—or if they do have children, will be bad mothers." [9]

As excellent and enlightening as Anna Fels publication is, her research, interviews, and analysis were done in the early 2000s, two decades ago. In the last twenty years, we can proudly say that women have moved forward and have gained confidence in our place and role in society. We have worked to reduce the 'ambition gap'. We see more and more women achieving more crucial positions in society. We see successful entrepreneurs with thriving businesses and families. But there is still a gap, and it is still big. Fels' words are still very relevant twenty years later: *"These days, the threat to women's ambitions comes at a later phase of women's lives, when they have families and are advancing to more competitive positions in their work."*[10]

In 2017, The Boston Consulting Group (BCG) conducted an extended research project titled *Dispelling the Myths of the Gender: The Ambition Gap.*[11] They analyzed data from two global BCG data sources and surveying more than 200,000 respondents. Their findings were clear: women start their careers with just as much ambition as men. Having children does not make women less ambitious, and women's ambition is largely influenced by the culture of whichever company that woman works for. *"Ambition is not a fixed attribute but is nurtured—or damaged—by the daily interactions, conversations, and opportunities that women face over time [at work and home]."*

This BCG study's clear outcome is that the culture and the workplace culture impact women's career ambitions. When companies create flexible workplace policies and positive culture regarding gender diversity, both men and women's ambition rise. "Women are ambitious, but they are also rational. If leadership looks attractive and possible, they want to be leaders. Otherwise, they may make the reasonable decision to opt-out."

Ambition and Gender Equality

The author of *The Other Half*, Simona Scarpaleggia states, *"One of the most common reasons employers turn down a female employee for a job, an opportunity or a promotion is not because she is a woman, but because she is a mother."*[12] I cannot speak about working women's ambition without talking about gender equality, specifically gender inequality.

Organizations like Advance, a gender equality institution in Switzerland, work on increasing women's share in management positions with clear strategies, tailored programs, and clear KPIs[13]. Without a structured strategy and commitment from companies, achieving gender equality will not be possible in the workplace. In spring 2020, during a writer's event, I enjoyed interviewing Scarpaleggia, the Manager of the Global Initiative for the future of our work at IKEA, co-founder of Advance, and a working mother. She said, *"Working towards gender equality is not only the right thing to do; it is also a smart thing to do."* In *The Other Half*, Simona explains not only why organizations and governments need to achieve gender equality; she also provides guidance supported by several examples and case studies. As of September 2020 Simona Scarpaleggia is the global CEO of EDGE Strategy, the leading global social technology solution for certifying gender equality in the workplace.

Many organizations focus their efforts on achieving gender equality. Countless books have been written on the issue. I am a fierce gender equality advocate. I consider gender equality to be my life mission and, as a life science and health care professional, my duty is towards patients in need. But this book is not entirely about gender equality and is not a "fix the woman" guide. After many years of listening to working women and mothers around me, I found the need to condense my findings and women's experiences in one place and share my knowledge and wisdom with anyone who is struggling with the same questions. When ambitious women become mothers, there is a big shift in their life; way bigger than what happens to men and anyone who does not acknowledge this would be wrong. We face more insecurities, more judgments, more pressure, and depending on where we live, where we work, and who we have married, it can sometimes force women to downsize their ambitions. The lack of gender equality both in business and society plays such a big role in women's professional lives that it is impossible to talk about one without mentioning the other.

Today, companies and governments have a huge responsibility to shape a new culture to enable everyone's ambitions to thrive. Gender equality is one of the biggest challenges in today's society and needs to be addressed. As Scarpaleggia says, *"There is a story that corporations all over the globe have chosen to ignore. This is the sum total of millions of lost opportunities because over half the potential workforce [women] was left behind."* [14]

A more flexible and inclusive working culture is a key element to nourishing women's ambition. But poor public policy and welfare, and the lack of cultural gender equality massively impacts women's ambitions and professional lives.

Christine Lagarde, President of the European Central Bank, and Erna Solberg, Prime Minister of Norway, wrote an open letter in 2018 to move governments to take action to increase women's empowerment and achieve gender equality. *"Almost 90% of countries have one or more gender-based legal restrictions."* [15] These restrictions range from women's inability to buy property to requesting a divorce. But there are some more subtle policies that impact women's economic empowerment and their willingness to stay in the workplace. An example is the Swiss taxation of a married couple, which provides a financial advantage to families with one revenue (usually the husband's), compared to families with double revenue (both working parents). Swiss families start to do their calculations as soon as they want to get married or there is a child is on the way, to see what makes the most sense for them. Unfortunately, families discover that often reducing women's employment rate is the most sustainable financial solution. This Swiss taxation policy is for many Swiss Gender Equality experts, including Prof. Gudrun Sander, the Director for Diversity and Management Programs at the University of St. Gallen, one of the main reasons many women opt for part-time work or stay-at-home solutions.[16]

The Staff Discussion Note of International Monetary Fund examines the effect of gender-based legal restrictions and other policy choices and demographic characteristics on female labor force participation.[17] Family-friendly policy both in the workplace and in society helps parents to focus on work. Still, it is imperative that governments *"strive to reform legal institutions, regulations, and laws to remove discrimination against women"* to enable *"the full potential of female empowerment."*[18] Ambitious working women are everywhere, and the context where they live and work plays an immense role in how they thrive.

"Helping women stay active in the workplace while raising a family is key."[19] In countries where affordable childcare and parental leave are a reality and policies support both mothers and fathers to work, women are thriving, companies are performing better, and society is more gender-equal.[20] In too many countries and companies, the full potential of women in the workforce is still untapped. It is up to us to reshape it and create a world that enables everyone to thrive and embrace their ambitions.

Motherhood and Ambition

On a sunny Saturday morning during the COVID-19 lockdown, I organized my first focus group about Motherhood and Ambition. The best way to investigate this topic is to ask mothers directly how they are dealing with their ambitions while their children are still at home and need their attention.

My focus group was aimed at mothers who had children under the age of five, which is when children require the most time, energy and money from their parents. I also found that it is during this time that most mothers make crucial decisions about their career and their future. Should I quit my job? Do I just work part-time? Should I keep my full-time job and hire a nanny? Can I afford childcare? Women with high education, a well-established professional life, and several objectives for their future face these existential questions while nursing their babies or organizing birthday parties for their toddlers.

I was looking for a selection of women representing the modern working mother in the Zurich area. My discussion group participants were six women aged thirty-three to forty-three, each having one to two children. Two of the six women were divorced. The group represented participants from several countries: two from Switzerland, one from Latin America, and three from other European countries. All of them were highly educated individuals with a corporate career and high personal drive.

DREAMS AND CAREER ASPIRATION
We began the focus group by discussing their aspiration as a young professional entering the workforce after university. I wanted to gauge when their ambition started and what influenced that ambition.

Interestingly enough, most of them did not have big dreams as university students. Most simply wanted to have good jobs and travel the world. However, there were a few women in the group who had extravagant dreams. One of the women told us, *"I want to become the CEO of a company."* Her ambition was and still is, fueled by family expectations. She and her family immigrated from Latin America. Her parents worked hard to be able to afford a prestigious education for her and her sister. *"I always knew I was ambitious,"* she said. Another woman in the group also had big dreams but was disenchanted after working in the business world. She told the group:

"I had this big ambition to be a strong and driven woman who could achieve whatever she wanted. I was determined not to care about other people but to be completely focused on my career goals. Now I work for someone who is exactly like that, and I don't like her at all. In hindsight, I realize that what I wanted at twenty-three was a fantasy. At the time, I was in business school, and everyone was ambitious. Now, I am asking myself, what is ambition to me?"

Many of the participants became ambitious after starting their careers. Their professional objectives became more precise and sharper while entering the workforce and learning what the world could offer them. One such participant said: *"I'm a very ambitious woman, and I knew it from the beginning. My country of origin provides few development opportunities compared to the rest of Europe. The first step was to leave my country, which would not provide enough work opportunities for me. My parents are very ambitious people and were supportive of my desire to study abroad. I decided to join an industry that would allow me to follow my dreams of traveling the world. I was open to any job proposals that would allow me to travel, and that would be good pay for my work."*

THE PARTNERS

The context we live in plays a huge role in our personal and professional life. Our plans can move forward, backward, or stop depending if we relocate, have the right life partner, or have the wrong manager.

While talking about our life context, one participant shared a very intense moment of her life. Her relationship with her then-husband (now ex-husband) was smooth until they became parents. He started to put a lot of pressure on her to stay home with her child. He would say to her, *"Don't you want to stay at home with your baby girl?"* She didn't notice initially, but he was bullying her, telling her to put her professional ambition aside and focus only on motherhood. At that moment, her company offered her a promotion with a chance to work abroad. Not only would she have built her career further, but she could also be able to afford to take the family away and give her husband a new opportunity in another country. This was the turning point of her marriage. Her husband did not agree with the decision to move, so they decided to divorce, as their life aspirations were diverging. She gave up her marriage and, unfortunately, also this job offer, but she followed her professional path and remained in the company.

"I'm in a moment where I understand I need to share this story. I want to tell other young women: don't let this happen to you! It is crucial to have the right person at your side! I'm still close to my family, and for now, the international experience is on hold. I know this is a barrier to continue my career."

After this intimate moment, the group supported her and agreed with her statement that having the right partner is crucial. He needs to cheer for you in your private and professional life.

"I was very lucky to find my partner very early in my life, and we were focused on adventures and develop interesting projects. I was driven by curiosity. I wanted to see different cultures. I never started my working life thinking, 'these are my goals.' I think because life was easy on me: no drama, no real problems, and money was enough to cover all the costs, there was no need to thrive. However, when I think back, I would have liked it if my master's professor would have told me to do a PhD. He never mentioned it, even to show me that career path existed. Maybe I would have done it. Now that I'm conscious that I missed an opportunity, I will talk to my daughter about professional ambitions early enough for her to not make the same mistakes."

If we all agree that one of the essential elements in our professional life is having a supportive partner, what happens if his life takes an unexpected turn, and you become the breadwinner?

"My husband is currently unemployed. And this makes my career ambition rise. I'm thinking about my next steps. How will I go back? How will I manage the kids? Should I go back to school?" At the time of the focus group, this participant was on her second maternity leave. She had noticed that this second break from work looked very different from the first one. She kept checking for updates from her company, was regularly speaking with her manager, and kept up with news and planning. *"It is a mindset. Of course, it is challenging, but we need to consider these first years with small children like an investment. If you don't invest now, you will miss your career later in life."*

CONTEXT

Sometimes a change of context is what we need to see all the opportunities we have or have lost. This could be a kickstart to your ambition, but it could also intimidate some of us or, even worse, put a stop to our professional trajectory altogether.

One of the participants shared her story on how she arrived in Zurich to work in a big consulting company.

"I come from an Eastern European country. I got the opportunity to go to Germany to study for a year and then decided to stay there. I wanted to do something nice and earn enough money to have a good life. I was very open, and I was thinking about majoring in music or philosophy. In the end, I choose business and economics. After selecting the best University in Germany, my biggest ambition was only to finish my degree. There were so many talented people around me. I did not think I was that smart. I thought I would be happy with my degree, and that's it. Then my husband and I moved to Switzerland, and this opened doors for new opportunities. I got a very good job at a consulting company with great development opportunities. My career ambition started when I saw all the doors open in front of me."

We heard just the opposite from another participant who said that the Swiss culture was an obstacle to her career path.

"For a long while, I did not like the country where I was. My husband was crucial to cope with the situation. I was not able to find a fulfilling job despite my qualifications and experience. I had an interview while I was eight months pregnant, and the human resources manager asked, "Why do you want to work? Stay at home with your child! You can afford it." I was shocked. Before that, I worked in the Middle East in some African countries. I traveled the world thanks to my job and got the opportunity to experience a lot of cultures. Switzerland is the

country in which I have faced and am still facing the most significant challenges from a career point of view, and such a statement says a lot about Swiss culture."

Others pointed out how the 'working culture' of a company is critical to their ambition or lack thereof. Many participants noted that flexible working hours, an understanding manager, and developmental options are all factors that increase their work happiness and ambition level.

"The employer is essential, and currently, I don't have enough flexibility to enjoy my family life. My goal is to increase my personal and professional network. This is crucial for my professional development and will help me find a new job too. I want to have a good job, and I want to stay with my kids. That means I need more flexible working hours. I know there will be compromises, but I also know I want more balance until the kids are older. I want to show my kids that it is normal for mom and dad to do what they like, both working outside of the home. I want them to know that this is fine, and we can 'have it all' so to speak, as long as everyone is happy and healthy."

THE MEANING OF AMBITION

We closed the focus group discussion with the last reflection about what ambition means. How do we feel about the word 'ambition'? Do we need to be driven women all the time? How are we evolving our professional aspirations with time? After two hours of getting to know one another, the women felt more comfortable speaking about their aspirations. While watching them from the screen, I regretted conducting this focus group during a COVID19 'lockdown' situation. I would have loved to have them sit with me over a coffee in a cozy restaurant and talk about their next big projects.

All of the women who attended this focus group defined themselves as ambitious women. But for every one of them, ambition had a slightly different meaning and intensity. Their meanings evolved with time and took on a new form after they became mothers. There were plenty of elements impacting their drive and professional achievements, both good and bad. One thing is sure: all of them keep their families at the center of their life while balancing their career aspirations. And this is the best we can do as working mothers.

Some of the women were very comfortable with being described as ambitious. One mother said: *"I have no problem with the word ambition and to be defined as such. This feeling evolved, though. In the beginning, I did not like it. But then, while working and meeting ambitious people and growing my ambition, I realized it is totally fine to be an ambitious person. My husband is also very ambitious, and we help each other in our professional life."*

Another mother said: *"I'm very comfortable with the word ambition, and I think it is very good to be an ambitious person. But it can be overstated. It is not fair to expect everyone to be ambitious. It is different for every person, and we should respect that."*

Some women mixed their ambition with their professional ambition and thought of ambition as a strictly personal idea shaped to their desires. One such woman said, *"What is ambition? For everyone is very different. For some, ambition involves salary, traveling the world, job title, good quality of life. Is it only the clichés? Everyone has their definition. For me, it is simple: I care about my salary, and I want to do what I want when I want."*

And still, others were not so comfortable with the mainstream idea of ambition.

"I admire people who are ambitious, who do everything to get what they want to achieve. But, sometimes, I just want to go with the flow and be. Other times I want to thrive, and I work hard to achieve what I want. I think this is also a good way to live."

Another woman noted how ambition changes as your life changes. She said, *"I was always a hard worker. Then I had a child and focused on what it took to have a happy life with my family. Then I divorced my husband. All these things aside, I'm an ambitious person. But in this phase of my life, I need to discover myself, understand what I want and what I need."*

A Personal Definition

I recall suppressing laughter as my colleagues looked at me with confusion when I told them loud and clear that I'm an ambitious person. One colleague has even described me as 'cold and calculated', a judgment which says that I am a career-woman and not a family-woman. Does this sound familiar to you? This description comes most probably from a misunderstanding of what I mean by ambitious. When I say I'm ambitious, I mean that I want to continue learning and developing new skills. I mean, I want to try new things, change roles within a company, work in a Non-Governmental Organization (NGO), write about working mothers, and build my own business. These are all achievements I reached because I pursued my ambitions while also fulfilling my role as wife and mother. Some have tried to guilt trip me for that, but I'm not ashamed of my ambition.

I have three principal life ambitions: provide a happy, sustainable lifestyle for myself and my family, enjoy a fulfilled and impactful professional life, and contribute to achieving gender equality. And because ambition is related not only to mastery of skills but also the recognition of what you've done.[21] At the end of my life, I would like to be able to look back and acknowledge my accomplishments. I want to be proud of the family life I have built, my professional achievements, and my contribution to the gender equality cause. Of course, part of my life's ambitions does imply a good paycheck, because how could I build a happy and sustainable lifestyle without it? It also implies that I need to achieve some level of leadership to have a fulfilled and impactful career. Nevertheless, my ambitions are related to my WHY rather than money or power.

As working mothers, we should not be afraid of being ambitious in all parts of our lives. We need to understand that our work defines who we are as much as our family and our interests. And there is no shame in that. At the same time, ambition is so different from person to person. We do not all need extravagant, complicated goals like establishing the next billion-dollar startup or writing a bestseller. Your objectives do not even have to be career-related. They can be things like creating equilibrium in your family, having a job that you love, being able to afford holidays in exotic places, and having a supportive network of friends.

I would like you to take a moment to think about the following questions.

What were your professional aspirations after you finished your education?

And what about your personal goals then and now? How did your ambition evolve with time?

Did your professional ambition change after you had children?

If yes, what changed, and how?

How much did your environment (family, culture, job) impact that change?

What are you doing to cultivate your ambitions and achieve your goals?

What are you doing to achieve your WHY?

It sounds like a lot of questions, but they are fundamental. Without a clear vision and goals in life, you will go nowhere. These questions are not only related to your professional ambitions. You can answer them when thinking about your personal, family and societal aspirations as well. Did you change your mind about how you'd like to impact the world around you after you had children? What are you doing to achieve your personal goals? What were your family aspirations when you were in your twenties? Heather McGregor, author of *Mrs Moneypenny's Career Advice for Ambitious Women* writes: *"There is no specific time in your career when you will need more, or less, help and support- at every age and at every stage women do better when they have the right ideas, the right focus and the right advice."* [22] Taking a moment to evaluate your life's ambitions and assess what you are doing to achieve them is the starting point of a successful journey.

My professional goals did not change after my son was born. And there was a large price tag attached to it. I had to pay high childcare fees and cope with comments like, 'How do you do all of that?' 'Do you ever even see your kids?' and 'When do you sleep?' Now I see that my husband made all the difference. He is way more involved in family and house activities than the average man. For my kids, their dad is emotionally, operationally, and financially just as supportive as me.

Realizing the uniqueness of my approach is the reason why I'm writing this book. I did not compromise in my ambition, self-development or my self-care.

I'm not a coach, and I don't want to teach you how to change your life. I would like to show you options and show you how other women face the challenge of being an ambitious working parent today. This book is the summary of other working mothers' wisdoms combined with my willingness to learn how to live a fulfilled life. Understand that you and I are not the only one with the **Ambitions Factor**, and you don't need to go through working moms' life alone.

Aurelie Litynski, Chief Happiness Officer & Founder of Happitude at Work, and mom of two girls provided me with a crucial insider's perspective. She helps companies increase their employees' happiness and has lots of experience on how people deal with happiness and satisfaction in the workplace.

There is no need to downscale your ambition. The country you live in, your life partner, your friends, and the profession you choose are factors that could influence this decision, but in the end, you are the one in charge of your life.

"Your happiness is your responsibility. You cannot wait for others to make you happy. They have a huge influence but the starting point is you. You need to know what makes you happy in your professional life; what's important for you and what are the drivers of your happiness at work. It is the same thing with ambition. Your ambition – Your responsibility. Only YOU can decide what type of ambitious women you are. There are many ways to be ambitious in life. You can be inspired by others but at the end you need to know what drives your ambition. What will you do with it? What kind of impact do you want to have and how does it make you feel?"

At the end of this book, I would like you to realize that there is no need to downscale your ambition. The country you live in, your life partner, your friends, and the profession you choose are factors that could influence this decision, but in the end, you are the one in charge of your life. Your ambition is like a child that needs to be continuously nurtured and rewarded. It will provide you with pride and satisfaction. And most importantly, ambition is not only about high paychecks, fancy job titles and business growth. The meaning is not the same for everyone, as every individual has their own drive, objectives, and life circumstances, which impacts the meaning of the word.

You are an ambitious woman, I know. Find what motivates you and find your way to thrive. If it is too difficult to find your aspiration or work for them, ask for help. There are plenty of coaches, psychologists, self-help books and websites, childcare options, and government assistance available to help you. You are not the only one trying to balance work and home life. You don't need to struggle with this by yourself. Now, I encourage you to go for it!

CHAPTER TWO

Don't Take Parenting Too Seriously

Valeria could hear the squeals of her children from anywhere in the house. The particularly deafeningly high-pitched squeal was her three-year-old daughter and the lower growl was definitely her six-year-old son.

"Mom! yelled the lower voice. "She broke my Lego car again!"

Valeria took a deep breath. **Can't they just get along for two minutes?** She thought with frustration. She had left them upstairs in their respective rooms to have some 'quiet time' while she tried to do about six different things at once in the house.

"Mom! She's destroying my things!" whined her son, reminding her not to forget about him.

She stopped doing her chores. She marched upstairs, dreading the mess that she might find there. The yells and screams were coming from her little girl's room. She opened the door to reveal a disaster zone! Her daughter had spread her huge bottle of moisturizing lotion all over herself and her room. The pile of Lego bricks were covered with lotion too.

"Mom! Mom! Look what she did!" He yelled frantically.

"That was not nice, covering your brother's toy in moisturizer," she said to her daughter.

"The toys were dirty, mama," she replied innocently, which made her son burst into tears. He then started to take her dolls and throw them on the floor. Valeria stopped him just in time to avoid more damage. Now both kids were crying hysterically. Valeria froze for a single moment, wondering how her life had become an endless series of childish conflicts.

"Ok, you need to clean up your brother's toy and then say sorry." Valeria took her daughter's hand and guided her to the bathroom and started to wash the Lego bricks.

After they were cleaned, she gave it back to her brother.

"Ok, now say sorry!"

"No!"

"Say sorry to your brother!"

"No!"

"You did something not very nice to your brother's things. Please say sorry!"

"No! No! No!" And she spiraled into a full scale three-year-old tantrum.

Valeria took her son from the room and left the little girl in there to express her emotions alone.

It took a while for Valeria to regain her composure. This was a lot to deal with after work, and with dinner not ready yet and a presentation for work to finish for tomorrow morning. **Where is he?** *she asked herself, referring to her husband. He would often come home late from work, missing the family prime time before dinner.*

Why isn't he here to help me? Doesn't he know how difficult this is? Maybe we should even think of getting some extra help in the evenings. Can we afford that? We need to talk! We need to distribute our responsibilities at home in a better way.

Valeria went back downstairs to continue her tasks, and couldn't help but think of herself as a failure as her daughter screamed and threw things at her door. Dinner was still not ready, the house was a mess and her presentation was waiting for her. Her career and her financial contributions were as important as the ones of her husband, but sometimes it did not feel like that.

I cannot do this on my own. I need help!

It Takes a Village to Raise a Child.

I remember when I first realized I was pregnant. I was scared and confused. It was never in my plan to be a mother of two. The ambitious girl in me was more interested in building a solid professional life than building a family.

Growing up in Ticino, the small Italian speaking town in the south of Switzerland, I had very limited interaction with my Brazilian family as a child. My Swiss family is a very small community of a few people that meet once or twice a year for Christmas and Easter. I have had the unique experience of seeing the European and South American perspectives of family life– which are quite different.

My Brazilian family, however, is a totally different story. My grandmother's home is the center of a vibrant and loud community. She had ten children, nine of whom lived, at most, twenty kilometers away from her. Her house was and still is the center of family life. When I visited my grandmother, her place was always busy with children running around, food, and people chatting in the living room. All the young mothers in my family lived nearby and had a great family support network to depend on. There is always someone checking in, offering to talk or bring food and solace. This mix of three (sometimes four) generations in one home was as normal as having the fridge stocked with food. This concept of *alloparenting* – when the care of children is assumed by a broad range of people and not only by the mother – is a reality in the Brazilian culture and benefits everyone.

Understanding my Brazilian family, you can understand the proverb, 'It takes a village to raise a child'. In this culture, there is no such thing as being alone at home with your newborn with only a midwife to check in on you a few times after the birth.

Let's face reality: modern (and urban) parenting looks very much like a solo job. If you earn enough money, you can afford childcare to help you with the essentials: care for the children while working during the day. No one brings you food, and rarely (if ever) someone shows up at your door, takes the baby for a while, and tells you to go and take a shower in peace. Nowadays, family and friends mostly check-in via WhatsApp or Skype. And no one asks for help from neighbors anymore for fear of looking like you can't do the job on your own. For those of us who are sharing our life with a loving and responsible partner, the responsibilities of keeping house and raising the children are equally split.

The evolution of parenting in the modern era and urban regions does not help young parents. And worse, instead of helping parents as culture suggests, technology enables parents to believe that they can do their work independently. You can find tons of content on websites, apps, and online forums to help parents cope with the first months and years of parenthood. This digital support grant parents to freak-out in the solitude of their living rooms.

Research points out that nowadays, parents are twice as involved in their children's lives and education than fifty years ago.[23] We are more worried about their physical and mental health. We ensure our kids have healthy hobbies, development opportunities, and steady social life. It is much more common for parents to send their children to see logopedics, phycologists, and other specialists to ensure their development is on track. We worry about what they eat, ensure they eat their vitamins, protect them from sun exposure, and select the appropriate gender-balanced toys. These things are all very recent.

Why do we feel that modern working parents take less care of their kids than a family with a stay-at-home mother? It's a mystery. No current data states working mothers are less involved in their children's health and development or that kids raised with both parents' working are neglected. This feeling is sometimes triggered by vague comments in conversation or the media. Despite the lack of evidence, it grasps new parents' consciousness like ivy on a fence.

MODERN PARENTING

Modern motherhood is a challenge. We are always judged and compared with some ideal models that do not exist. We need to find our way to be good mothers on our terms. So even if you and your life partner are both professionally active, think about different lifestyle choices or different ways of setting up your work schedule that can help you to be a dedicated parent. For instance, some parents live very close to work, limiting the commute. Some mothers have very flexible work schedules, which allows them to be more involved in their children's extracurricular activities. Some mothers are even able to work from home. We cannot put all working mothers in the same box just as we cannot put all kids in the same pot. Some children are very independent and prefer to stay with their friends and develop their personal skills in groups. Other kids need more time at home and more support from their parents (I will not include any reference here because, as a human being, we all know this is the reality). Every parent should decide what is best for their family based on their needs, personality, and circumstances, not based on their society's arbitrary expectations.

Modern motherhood is a challenge only if you keep looking outside and comparing it to others. My advice is, don't take it too seriously. You have everything it takes to do it well.

Are your kids happy, healthy, and well-fed? Do they have good cognitive and social skills? Yes? Then you are doing great.

Parenting is evolving. The home made up of stay-at-home moms and breadwinner dads was a model adopted by the middle class in the fifties by Western countries.[24] Today we can see different family organization models coming up. There are many stay-at-home dads and men taking paternity leaves. Dads are working part-time to raise their children. Many fathers are fully involved in domestic tasks, and mothers are chasing the next career step while having toddlers at home. We are slowly seeing a change of mindset, and people are becoming familiar with these new models.

One of the major factors contributing to the change is increasing welfare policies helping families and companies explicitly promoting women's return to occupational work.[25] Being a working parent today in Switzerland, Sweden, France, or the United States can differ. And considering the geographic mobility of corporate positions, many parents have firsthand experiences of the differences of living in a country with well-developed social-democratic welfare like Sweden or conservative regimes like Switzerland.[26]

This book speaks to all ambitious working mothers around the world. However, I need to place a spotlight on my lovely country, Switzerland. Someone once said to me, *"Switzerland is the perfect country to raise children but the worst for working parents."* I am not sure if it is the worst, but for sure, it is not easy. For a new parent, having children in Switzerland is excellent. Switzerland has a beautiful landscape, prestigious free education, and safe, clean playgrounds everywhere. As a working parent, especially a working mother, this view of Switzerland has changed for me. Switzerland is an expensive country, childcare for preschool children is a luxury, and after school activities aren't cheap. The public-school schedule and afterschool activities are impossible to combine with a regular working day. The taxation system seems to punish families where both parents are working, as the deduction for childcare costs is limited, and double taxation makes you rethink your married-life dream. When building their families and expecting children, Swiss families do the math and often come to surprising conclusions. Some couples decide not to get married but ensure that both parents legally recognize the children. In the case of married couples, women often opt for part-time jobs or stop working because, in the short term, this is the best financial (and least stressful) solution for their families.

Research conducted by Francesco Giudici and Reto Schumacher indicates several factors contributed to this so-called 'Conservative Switzerland' family model, where mothers stay at home and abandon their jobs after the birth of their first child.

"Why then, in Swtzerland, does motherhood cause a large proportion of women to interrupt their work or reduce their employment rate? Recent literature highlights a whole series of institutional factors, stemming at least in part from a long liberal tradition of non-intervention of the state in the private sphere: the care and education of children have long been considered to be in the private domain only." [27]

Many people who move to Switzerland from other countries come with this idea of a liberal, rich and modern country where they can raise their kids, work, and have a safe and comfortable lifestyle. During my years of intense networking in international groups, I always laughed at the recurring 'awakening moment' that happened when expat mothers realized that combining Swiss public-school schedules with their careers without the involvement of expensive child care was impossible. Many studies show that pursuing a career in Switzerland as a working mother is a big challenge.[28]

Despite all the challenges, plenty of working mothers living in Switzerland keep rocking their careers. Many elements play a role, of course, and their employer and type of business have a huge role to play. For instance, working for progressive corporations has some advantages. Substantial progress has been made in gender equality and work-life balance policies within some companies, making workers' lives better.[29] As a mother of two, I took full advantage of the flexibility my former company offered. Being an ambitious working parent in a society that enables you to be flexible and adapt your working time with your family's needs is better and more manageable than trying to thrive in your career and dedicate time for your family when your professional life is not flexible.

Interview with Kamales Lardi

If I had only three words to describe Kamales Lardi, they would be: assertive, competent, and sophisticated. When you first meet Kamales, the experience truly is something special. Even a quick discussion with her will make you understand that in front of you stands a unique woman.

I met her for the first time years ago at a Professional Women's Group of Zurich event, and I tell you, she was impressive. She was an engaging speaker, had an excellent presence about her, and was on top of her topic. For the entirety of the talk, she captivated the audience, and I was amongst the enchanted.

Years went by, and we met again on a few occasions. I invited her to come to one of my events to moderate a panel discussion about 'how to be successful online'. On this panel, she was insightful, competent, and sophisticated. I was impressed by her professional evolution and even more so when I found out that she is also a working mother. These two distinctions made her a top choice for my project, *Meet Another Working Mother*, for my blog, *Ana Just Ana.*

Let me formally introduce her to you. Kamales Lardi is the founder and CEO of Lardi & Partner Consulting, which is a consulting firm supporting and developing strategies in digital business transformation for companies; as an expert in digital business transformation, new technology trends, and social media, Kamales is very active in the digital world, is a keynote speaker, published co-author of *The Social Media Strategy: A Step by Step Guide for Building your Social Business*[30] and start-up mentor. She co-founded Diversity in Blockchain Switzerland. She is a mother with a multitude of business interests, and as such, I wanted to ask her what motivated her to do all of these projects? What follows are transcribed responses of Kamales Lardi from our interview in November 2018.

> Kamales: *"First of all, [my motivation] is passion. I love being part of the corporate world, especially now where traditional businesses are being completely disrupted. Challenging myself is very important too; putting myself out of my comfort zone and seizing new opportunities. I also want to show my child that she can achieve whatever she sets her mind to."*

Kamales has a daughter who already shows her strong character and her willingness to be different.

> Kamales: *"She is already starting to see that she is different. She is confident, and she wants to lead. She recognizes she not like the other girls at school. I'm very proud, of course! But I know it is going to be a difficult path for her, and I will be there to help her."*

In 2004, when Kamales arrived in Switzerland from Malaysia to be with her Swiss husband, it was a bit of a shock. In Malaysia, she was working for a global consulting company. She was an independent and empowered woman climbing her way up the corporate ladder. In Switzerland, she became "the wife of" – not even allowed to open a bank account without the signature of confirmation from her husband. Even though the legal requirement for a husband to cosign in order for his wife to open a bank account was abolished in 1998, the practise of requiring a husband's signature for forms related to opening an account, continued for several years. It has been a tough time, but she learned a lot through it. I liked how she turned her first challenges into strengths.

> Kamales: *"We cannot change what people think about us, but we can change our attitude toward their comments and reactions. I teach my daughter to be resilient and to follow her way, even if this means to be different than other girls her age. With my example, I would like to show her that she can design her own life as she wants and not feel constrained by boundaries that other people create for her."*

Undoubtedly, Kamales is a very elegant and feminine woman. Like many of us, she is a woman who takes care of her personal brand, not only with the work she delivers for her clients but also with the way she presents herself. I'm happy to know that Kamales, like me and many others, believes that being feminine is as important as the expertise she is bringing to the table.

> Kamales: *"I do not compromise on who I am, and the professionalism I bring to work is crucial. I work very hard to make sure we deliver what we have been asked to. I stick to my goals, and I strongly believe that the right attitude and mindset will take me where I want to be."*

Ambition Factor – Survey Analysis

After the Focus Group that I led, Ambition and Motherhood, I decided it was time to dig deeper into the meaning of ambition and what people think about it. As a scientist, my natural instinct is to pull together data to understand the world better. However, I lacked the necessary data to test my hypothesis.

Creating an online survey based on the discussion conducted with the previous focus group and the general idea and assumptions about ambition seemed to be a good start.

Being a pharmacist, I'm used to analyzing data coming from carefully selected patient populations and a controlled environment. So, I was skeptical about starting such a project on my own. It seemed very aleatory, from the question selection to the recruitment process. To reassure myself, I asked the opinion of some experts in surveys and data analysis. After obtaining their advice, I decided to launch myself into this project. The worst that could happen was that no one would take the survey, and I would end up with an empty online page. The best result would be to have enough data to see some trends and start a conversation.

The survey *The Ambition Factor* was online from May 14, 2020, to June 6, 2020. The survey comprised forty-three questions covering demographics (eleven elements), self-assessment (eleven questions), context (ten questions), and the meaning of ambition (five questions). There was space for participants to leave a comment at the end of the survey. The 163 people who participated in the survey were recruited via my personal network and social media. On average, they spent eight minutes completing the survey. I discovered only later that this survey was way too long. It took me weeks to analyze the data I collected.

THE DEMOGRAPHIC SUMMARY

164 people participate to the Ambition Factor Survey during 3 weeks in May 2020.

Gender

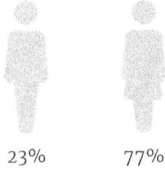

23%　　　77%

Age Group

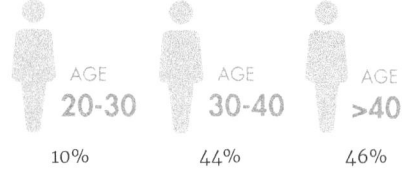

10%　　　44%　　　46%

Geography

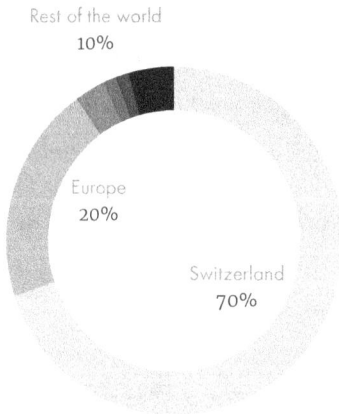

Rest of the world
10%

Europe
20%

Switzerland
70%

Education

Non-graduate　Bachelor-Master　PHD-MBA
7%　　　　　63%　　　　30%

Type of work

Employee　Entrepreneur　Unemployed
63%　　　　29%　　　　8%

Relocation

Never 14%

In the last 5 years 37%

More than 5 years 48%

Family Type

12%　　　38%　　　62%

Working Field

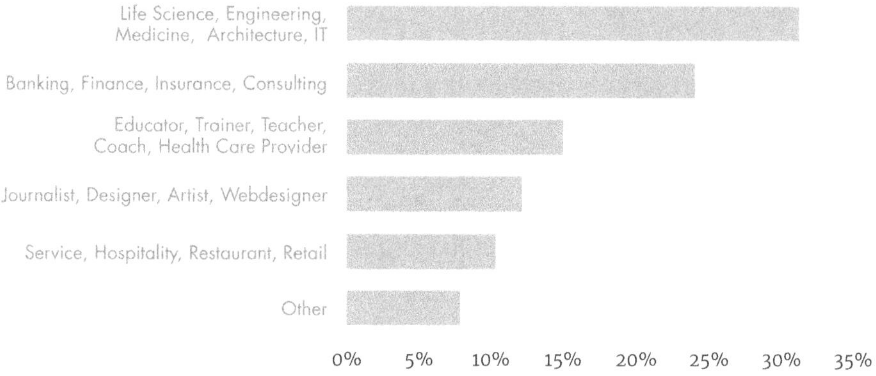
Life Science, Engineering, Medicine, Architecture, IT
Banking, Finance, Insurance, Consulting
Educator, Trainer, Teacher, Coach, Health Care Provider
Journalist, Designer, Artist, Webdesigner
Service, Hospitality, Restaurant, Retail
Other
0%
5%
10%
15%
20%
25%
30%
35%

ANALYZING THE DATA

While analyzing the survey results, I was reading the book *Factfulness: Ten Reasons We're Wrong About the World—And Why Things Are Better Than You Think* by Hans Rosling.[31] The book explores our misconceptions about the world by identifying ten instincts that mistakenly lead us to embrace an overdramatic, stereotyped, inflexible and unduly pessimistic view of the world. This book helped me to understand the data in a completely different way. In the first days, I was trying to confirm my own assumptions and misconceptions. I was sure there were substantial differences between women and men in how they responded to the survey. After reading the book, I decided to simply let the data talk.

Two lessons from the book were crucial to look at the result in an unbiased way.

The first was the importance of questioning the categories because they can be misleading. Rosling reminds the reader to *"look for differences within groups"* and *"look for similarities across groups."* As a result, I looked for differences within the group of working mothers analyzed the responses of women working in companies versus entrepreneurs, and not only working mothers versus working fathers. I made a special effort to look for similarities between different groups. For example, between the two age groups: the participants aged twenty to thirty and those aged over forty, regardless of their gender or family situation.

Then I needed to control my 'destiny instinct'. Rosling suggests, *"We tend to see things as unchanging, this instinct not to update our knowledge blinds us to the revolutionary transformation all around us. Society and culture changes and we need to adapt our world view constantly."* Remembering my experience with the personality for the consulting company, I had first-hand experience on how the "destiny instinct" played a role in the assessment of my personal thrive.

THE SURVEY RESULTS

This survey was a snapshot of the feelings and views regarding ambition and professional goals of people at the time of the survey. The survey showed very big differences between some groups, but gender was rarely the determinant factor.

From the very first question, "Do you consider yourself ambitious?" 80% of women and 90% of men said yes. The survey population was clearly the target group I was aiming for, and 10% difference is not that statistically important to make conclusions. The main gap in this first question and several others in the survey was between employees (employees and unemployed) versus entrepreneurs/self-employed. Almost all entrepreneurs/self-employed participants considered themselves ambitious (less than 3% didn't) compared 77% of employees and unemployed participants. These numbers are regardless of gender.

Education, work field or age group do not seem to play a big role either.

The following were the only outstanding results: out of 109 women only four highly educated mothers working in a company considered themselves as not ambitious. These women were the only ones in the whole survey population that did not assess themselves as ambitious people.

Taking a look into the difference between women with or without children or mothers versus fathers, the gaps are not that big either. There were three questions aimed at investigating the difference between mothers and fathers and their approach to their professional life:

1. Did you downscale (or will you downscale) your professional goals after having your first child?
2. Did your idea of ambition change since becoming a parent?
3. Are you prioritizing your partner's professional life over yours?

Here is the data:

Did you downscale (or will you downscale) your professional goals after having your first child?

	ENTIRE SURVEY POPULATION	MOTHERS	FATHERS	PEOPLE WITH NO CHILDREN
Yes, totally	6%	10%	0%	3%
Yes, in some extent	26%	45%	25%	6%
I don't know	26%	7%	0%	57%
Not at all	33%	39%	75%	11%
I don't plan to have children	9%	n/a	n/a	23%

Did your idea of ambition change since you became a parent? If you don't have kids, do you think it will change?

	ENTIRE SURVEY POPULATION	MOTHERS	FATHERS	PEOPLE WITH NO CHILDREN
Yes, it totally changed	11%	17%	17%	2%
Yes, my idea of ambition shifted and expanded	42%	57%	58%	17%
I don't know	24%	11%	0%	48%
Not at all	15%	15%	25%	14%
I don't plan to have children	8%	0%	0%	19%

Are you prioritizing your partner's professional life over yours?

	ENTIRE SURVEY POPULATION	FEMALE	MALE
Yes of course	8%	8%	5%
Yes, in some extent	13%	15%	11%
Just a bit	21%	19%	14%
Not at all	58%	58%	70%

In this survey population, the differences for these questions are not relevant enough to make any conclusion about the fact that working mothers relate differently with their ambitions compared to working fathers. However, it seems like women tend to prioritize their partner's career more.

Women's ambition does not differ from their male counterparts and their personal drive extends both in their professional and personal life.

Where your ambition is mostly focused on?

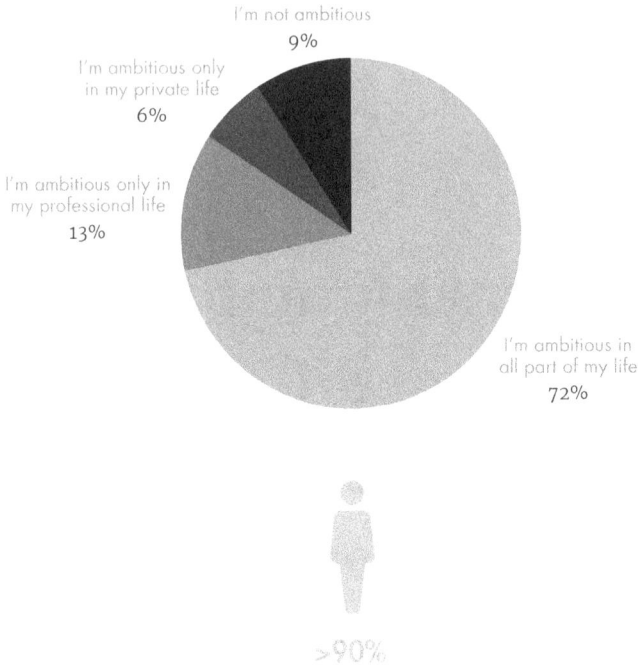

I'm not ambitious
9%

I'm ambitious only
in my private life
6%

I'm ambitious only in
my professional life
13%

I'm ambitious in
all part of my life
72%

>90%

More then 90% of people considering themselves ambitious,
extend their thrive in all part of their life.

If we consider the meaning of ambition today, we discover that, here too, the differences are very limited. Some 90% of people who assessed themselves as ambitious are ambitious in all parts of their life, not only professionally. Whereas, 40% of people ranked having a 'healthy balance between professional and family objectives' as the most important element of their professional life. This result is across all demographics and is independent of gender, age or type of employment.

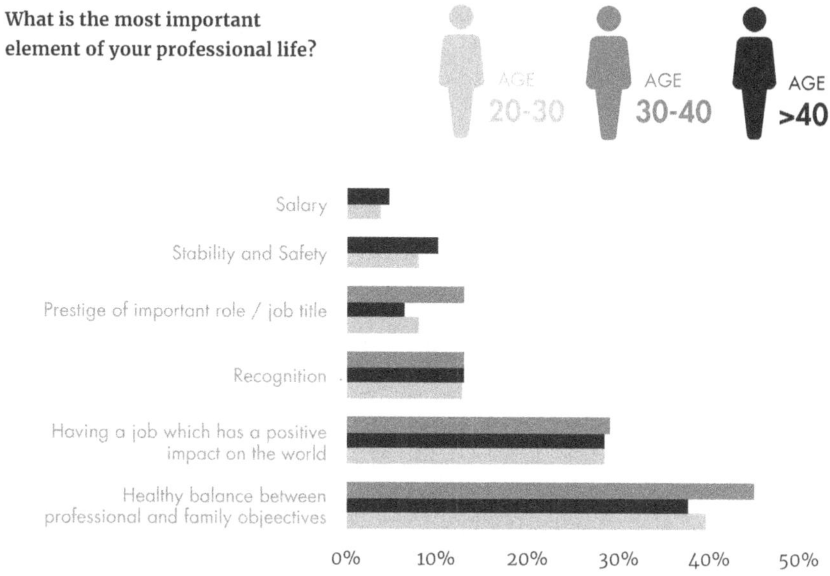
What is the most important element of your professional life?
AGE 20-30
AGE 30-40
AGE >40
Salary
Stability and Safety
Prestige of important role / job title
Recognition
Having a job which has a positive impact on the world
Healthy balance between professional and family objeectives
0%
10%
20%
30%
40%
50%

If anything, the results of this survey confirmed what I was thinking from the beginning: ambition, personal drive and professional objective are complex concepts that are shifting and cannot be generalized by gender. We cannot assess people's ambition only by thinking about their behaviors in the working environment. In a pool of highly educated, driven and professionally active women, this survey shows that children will most probably change and reshape the personal and professional objective set out for women and men.

The results agree with a similar survey conducted by BGC (Abouzahr, et al., 2017):[32] women's ambition does not differ from their male counterparts and their personal drive extends both in their professional and personal life. Becoming a parent, however, has an impact, but not in reducing the **Ambition Factor**. The impact is in shifting priorities and providing a new meaning. You can participate to this survey or learn more details in the website ambitionfactor.ch.

CHAPTER THREE

Take
Care of
Yourself

*Valeria opened her eyes from a long heavy sleep. She found herself tucked under
a blue woolly blanket and wearing nothing but one of those god-awful hospital gowns.*

I'm in the hospital... *She thought to herself, very confused. She tried to pull herself
up but couldn't. She tried to move her arms but felt the tug of IV tubes.*

*"You fell..." a voice answered her question before she even asked it. It was her friend
and coworker, Sarah.*

*"You fell right in the middle of a marketing proposal. You just collapsed! That mark
on your head is from you hitting a desk as you fell."*

"When can I go home?"

*"You need to rest. Look at yourself. You've got an ugly scar on your forehead, black
bags under your eyes and you are so pale. You need to take care of yourself!"*

"What about...?"

*"Your kids will be fine. They are with your husband. He can take care of them and
the house, you know?"*

*Valeria had worked too hard for too long without caring about her own physical,
mental or emotional health and she knew it. Her dedication at work absorbed
almost all her energy and at home she had no rest.*

Valeria's doctor had made it clear that she needed to come up with a plan for caring for herself before they would discharge her from the hospital. Her doctor had been frank, saying, "... if you do not make a plan for change, it's only a matter of time before this happens again..." A dreary thought, indeed.

Valeria sat up in her hospital bed, flipping through daytime television that she didn't ever get to watch. She began to see this time to herself as a good thing, a turning point, even though it had to be spent in the hospital. Valeria wondered to herself how every mother didn't find herself in a similar situation. **Isn't it true that all mothers put their children first before their own needs and try to do everything at home and work?** *She couldn't help but think of the women at work, who she knew were mothers. They all looked amazing, were in good spirits during the day, and led high-level demanding positions in the company.* **How did they do it?** *Valeria felt utterly burnt out and spent doing almost the same job!* **How could this be possible?** *She knew that she had not been eating well or exercising lately, always postponing workout sessions for a work or home emergency. And she had definitely been ignoring her mental health. Now she was forced to think up a new plan for her wellbeing.* **First of all,** *she thought,* **I need to find time for myself.**

She lay in her hospital bed with a pen and paper and started to plan.

Mens sana in corpore sano

The journey to become and remain an assertive, equilibrate, and an ambitious working mother starts with knowing yourself, your body, and your mind. Taking care of yourself is the central pillar of your success and the well-being of your family.

A French proverb is: *"Quand la maman va bien, tout va bien."* (When the mother feels good, everything runs fine). Self-care is as essential as taking care of your family and your professional life.

I am educated as a pharmacist. I know the biology of how our body works and how much our mindset impacts our wellbeing. And, in our day and age, holistic health is a very popular concept. So, we all know the basics of what we should do to keep functioning: a balanced diet, sleep, regular workout, outdoor activities, and keep a positive attitude. Despite this shared and public information, many people neglect their needs and end up burned out (or on the verge of a burn out) due to lack of sleep, lack of body activities, and bad nutrition habits. I'm not an expert on helping people find their balance and nourish their bodies and minds, but I recognize when it is time for someone to ask for help, and that is true of myself as well. I have learned to work with people who made it their mission to help individuals find their balance and live healthier lifestyles.

I would love to give you a quick three-step guide to follow to create an equilibrate lifestyle that allows you to thrive, but I cannot. There are many books already on the subject and a gazillion pieces of information on the internet. But I'm a pragmatic and practical being. Since you are here reading this book, I will tell you that it comes down to taking time for yourself. Yes, it's that simple. As mothers, we cannot function by only thinking about our children, partner, house, and work. Just as we ensure our kids have enough healthy food, sleep, social interactions, and fresh air, we should ensure all these things for ourselves.

It is a complicated and long journey where you learn to put yourself first. It should be part of our education as children, and we should grow up with this fundamental element to put ourselves, our bodies, and mental balance first. Of course, this implies knowing our needs and understanding how to achieve our balance. It is a lifelong odyssey, full of rewarding findings and new obstacles. When we become mothers, our natural inclination is to think of our children first. We are programmed to do so, of course, to be able to continue the human race and preserve the DNA. However, we quickly put our children's needs over our own, and sometimes this goes too far. I have witnessed mothers sacrifice their health and happiness for their families and end up burned out and frustrated. Every human being wants to be surrounded by happy and healthy people, so do our children. Why should we neglect our health and happiness?

I had the chance to meet some incredible (and ambitious) women very early in my life. These women inspired not only my professional drive and work ethic but my lifestyle too. Mothers and accomplished professionals, these women had one element in common: a sustainable lifestyle and a self-care routine that allowed them to flourish and keep thriving.

In my late twenties, I started to build a sustainable and happy way of living with my partner. Time for me, for my friends, playing sports, good nutrition, a fulfilling job, and purposeful nonprofit activity have been crucial elements in my life for years. I have the chance to be with my husband since I was nineteen years old, and together we shaped a way to live which fits our needs. When the children arrived, we adjusted our schedule, but the main pillars remained the same: healthy lifestyle, sport, nutrition, time for ourselves, support of each other careers.

I tell you what, it is a hell of a job! I feel like I am constantly scrutinized by people out there in regards to how I parent my children and manage my home. I am amazed by the number of comments I get! Comments like,

How do you do all that?
Do you even see your children?
Do you sleep?
When do you find the time to do all of this?
Maybe you are doing too much?

And guess what? No one asks those questions to my husband. Of course not. We have developed a lifestyle that is the best for ourselves and our children, according to our resources and time. We do not expect everyone to understand and embrace it. Wisdom has taught us to practice a more mindful approach to life too. We integrate meditation and nature activities into our family life.

Sport became very important only in my late twenties. Before that, I was finding every good excuse not to exercise regularly. I became an active dancer, and after the kids arrived, an active jogger. Exercising helps me to channel my energy and negative emotions. Often, I go for a run at lunchtime after an intense morning meeting. My afternoon mood always improves considerably. Some of the working mothers I've met and interviewed surprised me with challenging sports activities: marathon, mountain bike tours, or open water swimming competitions. I remain impressed by how some women manage to channel their ambitions, not only in their professional life but also in their sports activities. Their **Ambition Factor** is not confined only in their careers, it extends to their private lives too.

While recovering from the closure of my business Birdhaus, the coworking space I was forced to abruptly close due to the COVID-19 pandemic in

June 2020, and two months of being at home, homeschooling and caring for the children full time, my daily routine of craft training, running, and meditation were vital factors during my healing journey. During the whole COVID-19 spring, I was carefully paying attention to my body and mind. I integrated a yoga and meditation routine and a healthy food regime into my daily life (maybe a bit too much red wine, but hey, I had two kids under six at home!). Even with these things in place, I reached a point where I could not cope with all the stress and pressure. Looking at pictures of me at the end of May 2020, I wonder how I did not notice my pale face and dark bags around my eyes when looking in the mirror.

Several friends helped me understand how important it was to take a break and focus on myself. Two of them, working-mothers whom I admire, had experienced burnout some years ago. Both experiences were for different reasons and in different countries, but there was a pattern: they were both overworked and too focused on family needs. They neglected their body's need for sleep, equilibrate meals, and rest until it was too late. One told me:

"It took me two years to recover from my burnout. A new nutrition plan, workout routine, and a therapist were the pillars of my way to come back healthy and balanced. Now I know when to say "no" when it is too much and ask for help."

Meditation

Meditation is a personal journey. Everyone needs to choose what fits best for themselves. I cannot provide you with meditation advice. There are plenty of good guides, mentorship programs, groups, apps and websites to consult. I do recommend, however, to try meditation. In all my interviews and discussions with successful and balanced working mothers, many women practice meditation and a mindfulness routine. Practicing

As simple
as it sounds,
kids want
and deserve
happy parents.

mindfulness is a journey that requires time and commitment, as much as a sport does. The results will arrive slowly, but you will see how it has changed all parts of your life in the long run. I will be forever grateful to those who initiated me to meditation.

Several studies have been conducted to analyze the impact of meditation on stress, anxiety, and other medical conditions. Some demonstrated that meditation might decrease stress, especially in individuals with the highest levels of stress.[33] Another investigates the impact of meditation on holistic wellbeing in a work environment with healthy employees.[34] These findings demonstrate that a short program in mindfulness meditation produces demonstrable effects on the brain and immune function. Finding your calm and remaining focused even when everything and everyone goes wild at work and home is not easy. Meditation may help you to find more balance and focus to deal with these situations.

"Quand la maman va bien, tout le monde va bien." (When the mother feels good, everything runs fine). I would extend this as *"Quand les parents vont bien, tous vont bien."* (When the parents feel good, everything runs fine). As simple as it sounds, kids want and deserve happy parents.

Sleep

When I read about CEOs, top managers, and artists who wake up at 5 am to start their day with a workout and meditation, I shiver. I'm a big sleeper. I'm a night owl and hate waking up before 8 am (Ideally, I should wake up at 9 am even). Sleep is essential, and as a mother, it is one of those habits that dramatically changes after you have your first child. Sleep deprivation makes as many victims as bad nutrition because sleep is essential for our bodies and minds' well-being.

"[...] the cost of all those sleepless nights is more than just bad moods and a lack of focus. Regular poor sleep puts you at risk of serious medical conditions, including obesity, heart disease and diabetes – and it shortens your life expectancy. It's now clear that a solid night's sleep is essential for a long and healthy life." [35]

I have observed dozens of working mothers exhausted due to sleep deprivation. A former coworker was prescribed by her physician to sleep at least eight hours at night after a burnout diagnosis due to years of sleep deprivation caused by her son's lack of sleep. A friend of mine gained weight because her second child was not sleeping properly. She often found herself with her head in the fridge during these sleepless nights because she could not fell asleep. I have noticed this problem less in dads, though.

What happened in these houses where the kids are constantly waking up at night? A study conducted by Dr. Sullivan at the Jiann-Ping Hsu at the College of Public Health at Georgia Southern University in 2017, *Men with Children Sleep Fine; Women Not So Much*, analyzed data in the US population. [36]

Sullivan and her colleagues analyzed data from a nationwide telephone survey of more than 5,800 men and women. The respondents reported how long they slept each night, with seven to nine hours considered optimal and less than six hours considered lacking. The men and women also reported how many days they had felt tired in the past month.

Women with young children at home said they were tired 14 days a month, compared to 11 days for those without children in the home, the findings showed.

Among the nearly 3,000 women who were 45 or younger, the only factor linked with insufficient sleep was having kids in the house. *"Each child in the house increased the odds of insufficient sleep by 50 percent,"* Sullivan said. *"For men, we did basically the same analysis, and children had absolutely no impact on men [and their sleep]."* [37]

Unfortunately, the research could not investigate why the impact was on mothers only. We will leave this question open for the next group of research. For now, we will focus on the fact that mothers with small kids do sleep less than women without children. With this in mind, how to prevent exhaustion from sleep deprivation? That's simple: sleep more!

I know several mothers that when it became too much, they go away from the kids (and partners) for a couple of days to just rest and sleep. I remember hearing of one mother staying in a friend's flat while this friend was on vacation. This solution allowed her to go to work, and after work, go to an empty apartment, eat a takeaway and sleep a full night without interruption. My strategy is to sleep in the morning and let my husband take care of the kids in the morning. This is a personal choice of mine, which is only possible because of my supportive and understanding husband, who presumably needs less sleep than I do.

Sexuality

Let's be honest for a minute: sex life for parents is a taboo topic as much as money and salary. No one talks about it, but everyone would like to know how the other couples are doing. Often for parents, sex in no longer a spontaneous activity. It becomes an additional scheduled item to add to a very busy life. Unfortunately, often sleeps prevails.

While interviewing women for this book or my blog, I admit that their sex drive was never a topic of discussion (nor their salaries). Only with a few friends do I venture to talk about their sex life and even then, it is not very often. However, I can tell you what comes out of these discussions: the lack of sex drive is a reality for parents mostly due to stress, tiredness and lack of time.

People do not realize that our sex life is related not only to the quality of the relationship with our partner but also to our well-being. Several researchers point out how much a healthy sex life benefits our bodies (i.e. stronger immune system, better sleep, and cardiovascular benefits)[38] and our mental health,[39] by boosting our confidence and increasing happiness. And what about frequency? According to sex researchers, satisfaction and interpersonal warmth with the partner matter more in a couple than the frequency of intercourse.[40]

Experts say individuals can still have a happy and fulfilled life without sex, if they engage in activities that bring them pleasure like music or sports.[41] But for a couple, lack of sex life (considered less than ten times a year) has a big impact on their relationship and happiness and may lead to frustration and resentment.[42] Saying that, don't start to go all, *Fifty Shades of Grey* on your spouse to spice up your sexual activities after finishing this chapter.

Communicating your needs and desires remains the first step to building a healthy sexuality (and if kinky stuff is coming up in the discussion, go for it!).

HOW TO RELATE SEXUALITY AND AMBITION

A big revelation was speaking and working with Angela Ramel. Angela is an ambitious single mother of three teenagers, a Holistic Feminine Empowerment Coach, Tantric Embodiment Mentor, Master Hypnotist and Quantum Healer. With her holistic life coaching approach, she has helped thousands of ambitious women and couples from all corners of the globe and propelled them into higher stratospheres of connection, sensuality, energy and aliveness reclaiming their sexual sovereignty.

"From a young age, I had already experienced the power of the sexual energy to awaken, transform and accelerate my journey of self-actualization."

At the core of her work, she is here to support people in expanding their awareness and alignment of genitals, body, mind, heart and soul to enjoy more sensual pleasure and realize their soul's purpose. Angela's guiding vision is that: *"Our sexual power lies in knowing and asking for what we want, in knowing the resonance of our own hearts."*

When people start to understand that sexuality isn't only about intercourse, but about finding a deeper connection within ourselves, with others and with our vision, we unlock a whole new level of awareness. "We are hungry to feed the desire for deep intimate connections." When we are ready, open and receptive to deeper sexual, heart and soul connections, we allow ourselves to revitalize not only our intimate relationship but everything else in our lives, from career to bank balance. This new-found consciousness ultimately will help ambitious people to have a stronger relationship with their partners, friends and families, clients and business partners and will enable them to claim what they want and thrive in all aspects of their lives.

Nourish Your Body

Did you ever wonder why mothers take so much care of what their kid eats? Equilibrated meals, regular schedule, water, healthy snacks. Some mothers (mostly showing their **Ambition Factor** in their lifestyle) will even integrate explanation about the impact of food production, food waste and sustainability at the kitchen table. This begs us to ask the question: why do mothers not apply the same diligence and concern for what they eat? I reached out to a friend of mine, Sandra Mikhail, a dietitian specializing in gut health, and asked her for advice. Sandra helps patients find the best diet for their health issues. Sandra has over a decade of experience listening to mothers and excuses on why they are not taking enough care of one of their most basic needs: nutrition.

Considering the valuable guidance she shared with me, I have decided to integrate her words in this book. You can find her reflections and advice about nutrition and working mother in the 'highlight box'.

Nutrition and working mothers

BY SANDRA MIHKAIL

Working mothers already have it tough when returning to the workforce, yet the expectations that have been set on them have not only been confined to employment. From the moment of conception, moms are bombarded with opinions and judgments. Will you deliver naturally or opt for a C-section? Will you breastfeed or formula feed? Will you choose the baby-led weaning approach or go the traditional way? Will you give your baby jar food or baby food cooked from scratch? And the list goes on and on. So even when it comes to how you feed your families, a word of warning, expect more opinions and more judgments!

As women, we have been allocated multiple roles for centuries, and in older times, such roles were mainly cramped into the walls of a home. The mother, the nurturer, the caregiver, the cook, the cleaner, the entertainer, the wife, the pleaser. Amidst all these roles, the 'individual' gets lost. Women get pushed down the priority list and have been given the expectations of perfecting all these roles. You can see this when it comes to feeding the family. Add a role to the mix, i.e., corporate lawyer or business owner, the thought of prioritizing yourself becomes a joke.

The reason I wanted to highlight this before diving into the world of nutrition as a working mom is because every working mother that I have consulted has prioritized her family first before herself, not realizing that she is the core of it all. A healthy family unit requires an energized, rested and well-nourished parent. Many of you may see self-care as selfish, but truth be told, it is a necessity. So, rule number one when it comes to nourishing your family, remember that you are just as important as everyone else!

Nourishing your families, especially your children as working mothers, can become an emotional, physical and psychological hindrance. Before it turns into a weekly stressor, I want you to re-evaluate your attitudes and approaches towards food as perfectionism has even followed us into the kitchen. Once we've let go of this delusion, you can become more confident and comfortable around the food choices that you make for your family.

Below is a guide that I've been personally implementing for myself and shared with hundreds of working moms that I have consulted. Always remember to work with your reality, though and accept that there is no perfect diet, nor is there a 'one-size-fits-all' approach when it comes to family nutrition. Let's get into it.

1.
YOU NEED TO MAKE MEALS A PRIORITY

The 'let's wing it' attitude has caused so much frazzle and stress that if family meals are important to you, then you will need to prioritize some level of meal prep. Just like scheduling work meetings, completing your fortnightly budget report and so on, allocate a designated time in your work schedule to have a rough idea of meals to prep for the coming week. This can happen on a Saturday or Sunday but allocate about one to two hours.

2.
IMPLEMENT SOME MEAL PREP BASICS

Below is a beginner's guide to meal prepping:

Keep a pen and paper close by. So, you've got some meal ideas in mind and are perhaps aiming to try one to two new meals per week? Write down the days of the week and what you would like to cook for the next week or couple of weeks.

Think of categorizing meals or having theme nights, e.g., keep note of two pasta dishes, have a soup night, a vegetarian night, salads for lunches, etc. This may not be ideal for everyone, but theme nights are a big hit with families and kids, and you can get them involved in meal prep.

Write down a shopping list based on the ingredients you've extracted from the recipes. Having a list will prevent you from roaming up and down the aisles helplessly, help you buy the foods you need, and keep unwanted extras out of your cart. Also, set a day for your weekly shop, e.g., Saturdays or Sundays. Most importantly, take advantage of online grocery shopping!

I find it so much more efficient as a working mom, and I can repeat orders based on our previous grocery list. If you're one to do the reverse, i.e., shop for groceries first then look for recipes after then here's what I would suggest:

— Start with fresh produce such as fruits and vegetables. Avoid starting with the inner aisles and start by loading up on a selection of vegetables such as lettuce, cucumbers, tomatoes, baby spinach for salad ingredients and perhaps zucchini, eggplant, green beans, cauliflower, broccoli and asparagus for cooked options. Regarding fruits, go for lots of colors and choose blueberries, plums, peaches, passionfruit, strawberries and bananas, to name a few. Pick what's in season! Also, stocking up on some frozen fruit and vegetables can come in handy when your fridge is running low on produce, or you just lack the time to head to the shops.

— Don't forget about your protein sources. Ensure you're well-stocked on protein as it is an essential component of your main meal. Options to go for can include eggs, lean mince, salmon, skinless chicken breasts and for non-animal sources include tofu, tempeh and seitan as suitable alternatives. You can always add a variety of legumes to your cart, such as lentils, kidney beans and chickpeas. Dairy is also a great choice of protein, and getting small tubs of natural or probiotic yogurt can be a good addition to breakfast or even as a snack. Cheese varieties you can include and are not limited to cottage cheese, feta, goat's cheese and quark. Soy yogurts and soy-based alternatives can also be chosen.

— Stock your pantry up with high fiber starches such as whole grain pastas, brown rice (think parboiled brown rice ready in 10 minutes and NOT the one-hour kind!), barley and even grains and cereals such as quinoa, couscous and oats.

Get cooking! I'm one that likes the strategy of 'cook once, eat twice' and always plan for leftovers. You can use leftover chicken to add to a salad the next day or make extra batches of soup to freeze. Make sure you cook foods that tend to perish quickly early on in the week.

Keep track of favorite meals and start building a collection of family-approved dishes. In time, menu planning won't be a lengthy chore as your database of recipes and gold-star meals increases.

3.
BE STRATEGIC WHEN PUTTING A MEAL TOGETHER

Whenever you want to think of lunches and dinners, think of the three-step process:

Choose your vegetables and think of choosing three different types. Frozen, raw or cooked are all great.

-

Think about your choice of protein.

-

Pick a carb to complete the meal.

This list gives you an idea of choices, but please keep in mind that it is not limited to the foods mentioned. Also, portions of each will vary depending on the adult and child.

VEGETABLES (cooked or salad)	
artichoke	mushrooms
asparagus	lettuce/tomatoes/ cucumbers
green beans/snow peas/peas	
zucchini/squash	spinach/silver beet/ turnips
eggplant	
capsicum	cabbage/cauliflower/ broccoli

PROTEIN	
Skinless chicken breast	Eggs
Lean red meat (fat trimmed off)	Soy/tempeh/ quorn/seitan
Fish salmon/tuna/mackerel	Legumes

CARBOHYDRATES	
Wholegrain bread/Brown rice/wild rice	Barley/cous cous
Sweet potato	Corn
Rice noodles/wholemeal or buckwheat pasta varieties	Kidney beans/broad beans/ lentils/chickpeas

4.

MAKE PEACE WITH CONVENIENCE FOODS

Once again, this comes down to re-evaluating your attitude towards foods and 'convenience' options. There are many nights where planning has gone out the window, and you've only got eight minutes to whip up a balanced meal. Have a list of 'emergency meals' that you would resort to, and they can include:

— Frozen fish sticks and frozen sweet potatoes in the oven with chopped raw vegetables for a night of Fish and Chips.

— Ready-to-bake veggie burgers that are now widely available in stores. Have a quick read through the ingredients list and pick ones with the most veggies. You can add boiled eggs to the side of that.

— Ready-to-bake pastries such as samosas and spinach filo.

— Picking up a roast chicken on your way back from work and then adding some frozen veg and corn on the side.

— Bean stew using tinned beans, tomato sauce and frozen veggies. You can add any choice of carb on the side to that.

— Take out! There is absolutely nothing wrong with ordering in. You can set it as a weekly occurrence, and it can be the weekly pizza order (try to load on vegetable toppings). Once again, look at how often you've been resorting to take out. If it's more than twice a week, I suggest reflecting a little to see how you can adjust your weekly meal prep.

5.
COMMUNICATE AND DELEGATE

I think many of us may have issues with this, especially when it comes to anything related to the household and food, but as the saying goes, it takes a tribe to raise a family, and I say, take advantage of that! Ask your partner to be in charge of dinner once or twice a week and not comment on choice (I know it's hard but just let it go). If you're a single mom, ask for help from family, a friend or two that can cook batch meals for you to freeze. There's absolutely no shame in asking for help, and remember, we don't have to do it all.

6.
CREATE A 'HAPPY MEAL' WITH YOUR KIDS
(AND NOT 'THAT' KIND)

The environment in which you consume your meal is essential from when you are a child and all the way into adulthood. Mealtime should not be a negative experience for anyone. Ways in which you can create a happy meal with your kids include:

Getting your children involved in food, whether it is planning a special meal for the week, choosing vegetables when shopping for groceries or even arranging the salad bowl. Delegate tasks depending on age and get over the mess they'll make.

Never force-feeding your children and punishing them for not eating. If they do not consume their meal, just simply take it away and do not offer other alternatives. They'll come around eventually. YOU set the rules, and you SHALL NOT cook different meals to please everyone.

Encouraging them to try new foods and praising them when they do. When adding new foods, make sure you always include something familiar to them. It may take up to ten times until a child accepts a food, so be patient. Avoiding distractions at mealtime and sitting at the dining table and not in front of the television (whenever possible, and that doesn't mean never!). There will be nights where you just need the TV on, and that is ok. There is no room for guilt nor for mommy-shaming in our world so remember that even this dietitian had many dinner nights with the TV on. I also always encourage families to allocate two or three days a week to have a meal together. It doesn't have to be every night as for many families; this is unrealistic. Set a regular day if possible where the likelihood of consistency is high, for example, Mondays and Fridays are family weeknight meals together.

Ladies, remember that you'll keep redefining what healthy means to you and your families depending on the time you're going through. If you ever find self-judgment creeping up when it comes to how your family has been eating, first and foremost, remind yourself that FED IS BEST. Then, reflect on how you can tweak or manage mealtimes better without overwhelming yourself. If anyone has an opinion on what meals make it to your family's table, you have this dietitian's permission to tell them to bugger off. You will need to find the strength in you to block the noise, but when in doubt, there are many accredited dietitians and registered nutritionists out there that can support you. Seek, and you shall find us!

Sandra Mikhail

CHAPTER FOUR

Find Your Tribe

Valeria rushed around the house, trying to get as much done as she could before she went out that evening. Her husband would handle dinner and bedtime. *He is going to be ok with the kids, right?* Valeria realized that they still needed to redistribute more tasks at home, but this was a big improvement. Maybe he will even agree to have extra help at home?

She had been told to build a network of likeminded people who could support her and provide her with valid advice. So she was going to a networking event.

Valeria was not comfortable in large group interactions. She preferred to interact with a small group of people. She didn't have the self-confidence needed to thrive in big conferences. How can I connect with people I don't know? But all of her colleagues and even her supervisor were stressing the importance of networking to support her professional development. It was time to stop finding excuses not to do it and to start to connect with new people.

During her long stay in the hospital, Valeria had had lots of time to think about her support system or lack thereof. She realized that the only real support that she had was her husband and her friend Sarah who had come to see her in the hospital. She was beginning to realize that she needed more people around her. The other mothers at work did not manage their careers and family alone. They had mentors at work and help at home. Why should I do it all alone? So, she opened the door at the back of a restaurant down town and walked in. This was an event lead by a psychologist that gave practical tools for safeguarding one's mental health even through the chaos of today's fast paced lifestyle. Oh good, Valeria thought to herself, someone can help me to figure out how to work and raise young children without going mad. This sort of thing was exactly what Valeria needed.

The Right Partner at Your Side

The idea that you can have it all and do it all alone is a myth. I don't know who came up with it but believe me; if I find this person, we will have words.

Being a working parent while cultivating career ambition and a healthy lifestyle is a team game; you cannot do it alone. Don't get me wrong: we do not need to have it all, and for sure not at the same time. There are several ways that you could do this:

You could choose to have a rewarding
professional life and a family in balance

-

Dedicate your time to building your family
and a healthy lifestyle with a less demanding job

-

Stay at home and focus on your family
for a while and go back to work later

The choice is yours. Still, you cannot do it alone.

To have a normal and equilibrate life, we need to have as much support as we can. Some of us are lucky to have grandparents and aunts and uncles who live close by and help out. But some of us don't, myself included. In this situation, we need to carefully organize our lives and make critical decisions to guarantee peace of mind and avoid burnout.

DON'T TRY TO GO IT ALONE
When my first child was born, my husband and I decided to put him in childcare and pick him up in the evening, like millions of other couples. At the time, both of us worked about forty minutes from home. We were either

stuck in traffic jams during our commute or had last-minute meetings to attend. After finally arriving at the daycare to pick up our son, we went home very stressed out and in a rush to make supper while the baby was crying. It did not take us long to understand that this was not the kind of life we wanted ourselves or our baby. So, after a month of chaos, we hired a nanny who picked him up after daycare and prepared our evening meal for us. As a result, we came home less stressed and found our little boy happy and relaxed.

It occurred to me that this solution was great for everyone. Of course, it comes with a high monetary cost. Childcare and nannies in Switzerland are both luxuries. We could afford such a solution because we both had good jobs. But what was the cost of not doing it? Somehow, I never felt that I needed to try to do it all by myself. I have always believed that I have qualities and strengths that are better used outside of the home. I was not built to be content with cleaning the house, preparing all the meals, and staying home with my children every day.

Now don't get me wrong. Of course, I love my children, and I am meticulous in my care of them. I always ensure my kids are taken care of, the house is clean, the fridge is full, everyone has healthy meals, and that the children are engaged in social and outdoor activities. But this ability to manage so many facets of my life requires attentive scheduling and a lot of people around me. And the same thing goes for my work life, my work with an NGO, and my entrepreneurial activities.

There is no objective I have that I have reached or will reach alone.

But, there is a BUT. There is always a 'but'. The balance and harmony that I have achieved with my family are possible only because I have a great husband by my side.

"The prioritization of career within a marriage is one more barrier to the ambition that we observed among our friends. [...] We believe it is important that women recognize this phenomenon and understand that there is deeply internalized belief shared by both men and women that a wife's career is less important than her husband's." [43]

As Shank and Wallace observed within their sorority group, several women put their professional ambition aside to benefit their husbands' careers. The High Achievers, the highly ambitious mothers with accomplished careers, on the other hand, did not. *"They took charge of their careers but also chose partners who supported their goals and shared family tasks."*

Avivah Wittenberg-Cox is CEO of 20-first, one of the world's leading boutique consultancies and a regular contributor of HBR. As a worldwide recognized gender equality advocate, her articles and speeches always go to the point with crystal clear statement. Her research and observations of dual-career couples have a great deal to teach us.

In her article, *If You Can't Find a Spouse who Can't support Your Career, Stay Single,* Wittenberg-Cox puts it in an even more simple and clear statement: *"Professionally ambitious women only have two options when it comes to their personal partners – a super-supportive partner or no partner at all. Anything in between ends up being a morale- and career-sapping morass."* [44] In Sherly Sandberg's book *Lean In Women: Work and the Will to Lead* you find the same conclusion: the most important decision to a woman's career is who to marry.

Open conversations, planning, shared family tasks, common long-term vision, and respect for both careers and personal objectives are key elements to allow ambitious working mothers to thrive. These elements are built with time and with the right partner. [45]

Some years ago, I interviewed Barbara Stupp for my blog, *Ana Just Ana*. Barbara´s daughter recently left home to start her adult life. Barbara is no longer in the phase where she has to juggle childcare, nanny and unplanned fever episodes. She is in the phase where she again organizes her daily life without worrying (too much) about her daughter. She shared her wisdom.

"The biggest change was not to have any time for myself. I had always had the wish to combine work and motherhood. I need the recognition of achieving results, and I just knew that a 100% focus on my child would not make me happy. In retrospect, the key to make this combination work for me was a partner who supports my desired way of living. I needed a husband who does not 'help' me but wants to share the home duties and home pleasures. Sharing responsibilities at home was a hurdle for me because it meant losing control and letting my husband do certain things his way. It took a while to acknowledge that I had to become flexible on how things were done at home."

Lives evolve, and relationships can come to an end for various reasons. Suddenly parents are raising their children from separate households, and new routines start. One recurrent topic which comes out while I talk with divorced (or separated) mothers is that they had newfound time for themselves. With the kids away from home on the weekend or part of the week, it seems that many mothers discover the joy of precious time for themselves, which was forgotten during their marriage.

It took me a while to understand why this particular element of the divorced life kept coming back to my mind. I arrived at my "Aha!" moment while I was explaining to a divorced mom how I managed to organize my life with two kids, a full-time job, and an NGO to lead. *"I would never have had the time to do the NGO tasks and networking as much while I was married. I cannot imagine how my husband would have reacted if I was away from home in the evenings."* Her comment triggered something in me: delight and pride to have a great partner at my side, and sadness after realizing that some partners are not as supportive. The lack of support in the family organization by their partners impacts mothers and their ambition big time.

CREATING GENDER EQUALITY IN YOUR RELATIONSHIP

One of my favorite self-development and empowering books is *Drop the Ball: Achieving More by Doing Less* by Tiffany Dufu. I could not put her book down because I had the feeling she was describing my life most of the time (minus her being a famous celebrity). As an ambitious, high achiever, NGO leader, author, wife, mom of two, Tiffany is a role model I look up to. Her book, which is part self-development and part memoir, describes everyday situations she experienced with her husband and children. She provides great advice on how to 'Drop the ball' at home and work and how to focus on what matters most. One piece of advice I implemented in my life as soon as I finished the book (and I keep recommending to most of my friends) is Tiffany's Home To-Do list – MEL (Management Excel List). The whole chapter, 'Clarify Who Does What', makes the entire book worth buying and reading. It is so funny, so real, and so needed.[46]

She created a spreadsheet with four columns: one for all the tasks that need to get done to keep the household running, one for items she would handle, one for items her husband would handle, and a column that no one would handle – things that could be skipped completely.

It took me a while to grab the courage, sit with my husband, and perform the same exercise. We enjoyed the exercise as scientists who were very familiar with using Excel files. It was a revelation. We discovered that to run a house, take care of two children under four while having two highly demanding careers, NGO commitments and sports routines was a very big job. Our column four was not 'Drop It' but was 'Delegate It' (Dufu, 2018). We included a nanny, cleaner or any other person who could handle tasks

Achieving gender equality in your spousal relationship is imperative. Only then can you both cultivate your ambitions and have a fulfilled life.

for us. And to use Tiffany's expression, we "delegated with joy!" Once we finished the list and assigned clear responsibilities following our skills and talents, our accountability to our tasks changed. For instance, I no longer thought about the tax declaration. It was decided that my husband would tell me what he needs from me to do it on time. And he no longer thought about health insurance, physician bills or the children's appointments, as that was on my list of responsibilities. We do not follow-up constantly on each other's tasks. We do not resent the other for "not thinking about doing that task", and we don't worry that something is not done because we fully trust the other to take care of their duties.[47] Of course, it is not always easy. Some activities need to be shared, and others cannot be included in the list. And in every couple, there are moments we fall into passive-aggressive, resentment or punishing behaviors. For example, there is yet another load of laundry to be done. He never sees it! Everyone creates dirty laundry so this should be a shared task! If I ever stopped doing the laundry, he would understand how quickly the clothes accumulate in the dirty laundry basket. When faced with these situations, we discuss the issue before it escalates. In this case, I would tell him when to load the laundry and fold the dry clothes because he really does not see that it needs to be done (still a work in progress). Another example: I expect my husband's calendar to be flexible and fit all my social engagements, even the ones that are short notice. If an invitation for an event comes up at the last minute, I need to accept I may not be able to go to it (I'm still working on this one).

When I describe this exercise to some of my friends or acquaintances, I get very different reactions. Still, the most frequent is: "Not sure if my husband could handle having our whole life described in an Excel spreadsheet." My friend N. told me that a friend of hers did a very similar exercise when she divorced her husband. They both had very demanding jobs and a child involved in many school activities, so they needed a clear distribution of tasks and responsibilities. As a result, her friend felt less stressed and trusted her ex-husband more than when they were married. After her friend's revelation and my description, my friend N. seriously considered talking her husband into building such a list for their family.

Sometimes we forget that professional life is a long marathon and not a sprint. For both men and women, we cannot always be in the accelerating line where we need to give the best of ourselves. There are moments that we can cruise, enjoy our acquired comfort zone, and dedicate more time to our life beyond work. This situation may happen when one in the couple needs to push for the extra mile, while the other can dedicate more time to the family. Living as a couple is an evolving exercise. We need to keep assessing the situation and paying extra attention to changing needs, both personal and professional (and eventually change the task list to accommodate the new routine). As I've said earlier, being supportive and understanding are key factors and it needs to be mutual. For me, there is only one key element: we need to be equal. Achieving gender equality in your spousal relationship is imperative. Only then can you both cultivate your ambitions and have a fulfilled life. And achieving gender equality in the couple will lead to gender equality in the workplace and in society. The right partner at your side needs to embrace gender equality, and his action, not his words, will show this to you.

NOT THE RIGHT ONE

But what happens if the partner at your side is not the right one? I interviewed several divorced or separated mothers for my blog and this book. It is painful to listen to their stories of unrealized ambitions and life goals due to their separation. In many cases, separation or divorce had a massive impact on their professional life. Not surprisingly, ambitious working mothers had this extra drive to prove they could keep a rewarding job and raise their children despite the separation. When I approached the topic of professional ambition with divorced mothers, I was afraid to go into 'No Man's Land'.

In their stories, there is sorrow, strength, courage, and, most of all, resilience. I have learned that the life of a single mother is scary, but it does not have to translate into leaving all your lifelong ambitions aside forever. Mostly it is about taking a break, finding a new balance, and starting to thrive again when you are ready.

A Tribe of Women is the Best

One of the smartest things that I've done for myself is to join the Professional Women's Group of Zurich (PWG) very early in my career. I was twenty-seven when I started to enter my first networking events. PWG was known to provide quality events around the topic of professional growth in the city.

Event after event, I have met amazing women, ambitious professionals, of course, who helped me understand what matters in my professional life, how to shape it, and how to recognize what was right for me. In my early days of networking, the main messages were: delegate when possible at work and at home, work as a team, and ask for support. I religiously applied these principles and kept doing it in every part of my life.

Joining and supporting a women's community in the early years of my career allowed me to meet many ambitious women of all kinds: entrepreneurs, bloggers, fashion stylists, high-level executives, government representatives, academic representatives and visionaries. With time I understood that success is not what makes most ambitious women thrive. Having a positive impact on the world and having a happy family life were the key factors that fueled their drive. That's why I do not connect ambition with success, money, or power. Purpose and happiness are both motivation and objectives of my ambition.

FIND YOUR TRIBE

Find a tribe, a group, a community in which you feel comfortable, energized and understood, in which you share the same values and where purpose sounds like a life quest. Nowadays, we can even join virtual organizations, Facebook groups, Instagram pages; the options are endless. Despite the ease of joining a virtual community, I still recommend joining a physical one. Meeting and talking with other women in a cozy and safe environment after an inspiring presentation is priceless. Joining a group will allow you to expand your network, which is a crucial element for your professional growth. Once you have found a group that you like, please be sure to invest time in building those relationships. It will be worth it in the end.

Here are some suggestions for ways to connect with the women once you have found 'your tribe':

Ask the group organizer if they need help. Most of the women's groups worldwide are run on a volunteer basis, so free help is always welcome.

−

Ask questions and make suggestions for the subject matter. If you find a particular area of life that you are struggling with or are interested in, ask the organizer to speak to that or arrange for a speaker.

−

If you feel comfortable sharing some of your wisdom and knowledge, then offer to present it to the group.

−

Challenge yourself by speaking to all of the women in the group, despite their various professional titles or titles within the group. When I was president of a women's group.

I found that some people were afraid to talk to me or ask me for a coffee because I was 'The President'. I realized that sometimes titles and achievements can be a bit intimidating. There is no need to be afraid; we all want to help and support each other.

There are so many benefits to joining a local women's group that meets in person. Here are just a few:

Sometimes, you don't know all the strategies available to cultivate your ambition and organize your life accordingly. Talking with other women you admire who you think are doing an excellent job managing their professional and personal life could help you considerably. Everyone has their own strategy, and maybe you can learn one trick or two. Perhaps they went through the same pain as you did, and they found a solution you do not see yet. Or maybe you will share the solutions you found.

You establish a support system of women who understand the chaos of your life because they are dealing with similar things.

I have always said that it is healthy to get out of the house and have a much-needed break at least one evening a week, so this is a good excuse!

By joining an established group, you will find many women who already have a certain level of seniority, maturity, networking, and self-awareness. You will contribute and support this tribe with your personality and experience too.

The benefits of joining a women's club and finding your tribe are endless. Look for a group that would be the right fit for you and challenge yourself to engage. There will be many benefits to reap. I promise you!

FIND THE TIME

Most of the networking events in urban areas are during the workweek, directly after work. Many women joining such events are mothers, and this says something. Their partners are taking care of the kids, the dinner, and bedtime. You would be surprised how many mothers I have met over the years that refuse to go out in the evening because they don't think their partner can handle caring for the children, making dinner, cleaning up and putting them to bed. I have heard the excuse *"I have no time for networking"* time and time again. But, you have to believe that the children are just as much yours as they are your partners. He can take care of them! Release yourself! And if you really don't think he is capable, then hire a babysitter for an evening. I have found that women who make time for conferences and networking events understand that their own self-development is important too.

I want to stress the expression: **make the time**. There is not such thing as *"I don't have the time."* You may think that people with a family and a demanding career have absolutely no time to spare. Maybe you do not see the full truth. Just like we find the time to engage in sports and social life, we need to schedule our week, family calendar, and work tasks according to our needs and priority. Laura Vanderkam, the author of *I Know How She Does It: How Successful Women Make the Most of Their Time*, reveals how ambitious and successful working mothers make the most of the hours they have in a week. She did an experiment with 143 women for 1001 days. The women selected were high achievers and had at least one child under the age of 18 living at home. Vanderkam requested time log diaries with details to understand how these women open their days.

Vanderkam, an ambitious and successful mother of four, breaks the myth that working your way up the career ladder means tremendous sacrifices of time in regards to your personal life. The data she collected shows that with the right time management skills, clear priorities and flexible working hours, you can build your career, have quality time with your family and have some fun too. Her mantra is: *"... time is highly elastic. We cannot make more time, the key is time management of our priorities."*[48]

THE POWER OF A 'FIXED NANNY'

I'm a strong believer in having one 'fixed' nanny whom you can call upon to help when necessary. Having a fixed nanny in place goes a long way to ensuring that you have some time to devote to your own social, emotional and professional needs. From the beginning, this helped my husband and I to be less stressed about our working schedule, business travel, kids' illnesses, and last-minute disasters (there is always an unexpected disaster of some kind). One of our guiding thoughts while planning our children's daycare is thinking of it as an investment and not a cost. My husband and I understand that our jobs give us the benefits of such a choice. Considering the high cost of childcare, not everyone can afford this way of organizing their family life.

I know plenty of couples who manage by themselves without having a nanny, some better than others. In my opinion, every family choice comes with a cost. If a couple decided to do everything by themselves and didn't try to make time to work out or spend quality time with friends, that is fine. The important thing is to make sure that you or your partner do not become resentful or frustrated.

Having someone other than the children's father to help you with caring for the children can completely change your home life for the better.

HAVE PLAN B IN PLACE

Some studies pointed out that in the workplace there is this belief that women with kids are less committed to the job. It has been suggested that overall they work fewer hours, work part-time, and stay home when the kids are sick. Jan Williams' *The Maternal Wall* (a term referring to stereotypes and various forms of discrimination encountered by working mothers) describes a reality in many workplaces, and most of us are facing it without knowing it.

"Women who have been very successful may suddenly find their proficiency questioned once they become pregnant, take maternity leave, or adopt flexible work schedules. Their performance evaluations may plummet, and their political support evaporates." [49]

All high achieving mothers I have interviewed told me the same thing: having a back-up plans to deal with unexpected situations is imperative. Being a professional implies you will inevitably have conflicts with your job and your family duties. In order to be more successful and less stressed out, you should have a system in place to deal with these unexpected situations.

Here is a short summary of some practical strategies:

Speak with other working mothers, especially those in high up corporate positions, and ask them how they deal with these unexpected situations. How do they balance or prioritize? How is their home organized?

–

Open communication with your partner. Talk to your partner about potential scenarios that could happen while you are out at a networking event or a professional conference. Plan ahead.

–

Think about restructuring your family organization. Is the current way of doing things the best way?

Understand that every single household is different. There is not a 'correct' answer. You need to come up with your own strategies that will fit your family's unique needs.

Two years ago, I met a working mother who relocated her family from a Nordic country to Zurich. Her career brought her to Switzerland. Her highly demanding career with an insurance company was on the rise. Her partner was a stay-at-home dad. While at home, he focused on sports, freelance activities and organized his schedule according to his kids' and wife's needs. They had a house cleaner and nanny, allowing him to take time for freelance projects or go to networking events. The only complaint I ever heard from him was at the playground, when he said: *"There are almost no dads in the playground during the week."* When the youngest child turned three years old and went to childcare, her partner started looking for work. Still, he remained the primary caregiver taking care of the children when they were ill. The couple arranged that the grandparents would be called upon to help if his workload became too demanding. She travels too much and has very limited flexibility to work from home.

The point is, this family built a life that worked for them and had in place strategies to deal with their professional lives. They anticipated their needs and had a support system in place for those unexpected situations. Many of these situations involved carefully planned home logistics, reliable support, and clear communication. And most important, a solid vision of their lives and careers.

BUILDING YOUR TRIBE IS CRUCIAL
FOR YOUR MENTAL HEALTH

The legendary Greek philosopher Aristotle said, *"Man is by nature, a social animal."* [50] We are not made to live isolated. Friends, social connections, and family are as important as our occupation and health.

My experience in building my tribe started when I moved to Zurich from Geneva. Relocation forces people to network, as one usually does not have friends or family in the place they are moving to. My relocation involved learning a new language. For the first years in Zurich, my German was far from fluent. But regardless, I knew that I needed to create some connections. My first networking events were with groups of people who spoke Italian, French and English, the three languages that I am most comfortable speaking. Meeting people who spoke my languages (and struggled with learning German) helped me to connect quicker and start to build a new circle of friends.

Looking at the people I admire (men and women), they all have a solid group of friends supporting them. Personal and professional development drive people in a specific direction. Often, people surround themselves with people who embrace the same lifestyle choices.

The best thing for you as a working mother is to surround yourself with other kick-ass working mothers. I encourage you to look for strong women who are building their life with definite goals, who have your back when you are in need, and who will lift you when you are at a low point in your life. Women with the **Ambition Factor**. Learn from these women and lean on them. Find out how other mothers cope with the chaos of balancing home life and work life. Share ideas or just plain vent to them over a glass of wine after a long, frustrating day. You need to have someone in your life who will listen to you and who can completely understand what your life is like and who understand what you are doing and why you are doing it.

I will say it again, find your tribe. Connect to your tribe. Your tribe is crucial to your mental health and your very survival as a working mother.

Five Golden Rules for Mastering Your Networking Skills

Part of finding your tribe is having a willingness to network with others. Despite common thinking, networking is not only about going to events, engaging in some small talk and exchanging business cards. Networking is about creating meaningful and authentic connections with likeminded people. What do you want to achieve with these connections is up to you.

My experiences of leading a professional networking group have shown me that networking has some basic rules. I have started to share these principles in keynote speeches and what surprises me the most is, despite the simplicity of these rules, people do not seem to be aware of them.

These tips will help you master your networking skills, enhance your ability to connect with people, produce growth both personally and professionally, and cultivate your ambition.

Find Your Networking Style.

If you want my advice, I would suggest that you answer these three questions before you sign up for a networking event:

Why do you want to network?
It seems like a silly question, but it the most important. Are you new in town and want to build new friendships? Do you want to change your job and go to another company? Do you need clients? Do you want to develop more contacts within your company? Understanding what your motivations

are will push you to increase the number of your contacts you make. If you just recently moved to a new city and want to hang out or meet new friends, go to yoga or a dancing class. On the other hand, if you are looking for a new job, groups (digital and face to face) in your sector of interest and or for people working in that area, LinkedIn might be the best option. So find out why you are networking and make sure that whichever event or strategy that you are implementing meets that goal.

What Are Your Challenges?

Everyone has challenges. Here some examples: you might have a small child who needs childcare, which makes an evening networking event very difficult to schedule. Shyness and fear of a big crowd is a major issue. A language barrier can also be an obstacle to overcome. An accurate analysis of your challenges will help you to pick the right networking options that fits your needs.

Once you have figured out your objectives and your challenges, you can start looking for the best networking solutions. You can start with the classic organic search. Social media is one of the best channels for looking for groups and people of interest. Pay attention to the quality of the group and who is organizing it. In big cities, there are so many, and the challenge is to pick a good one. Another channel to look into is a one-on-one meeting. They are very effective in building authentic and meaningful relationships. With social media, especially LinkedIn, it is so easy to look up people working in the same field or having the same interest. Direct contact and a follow-up call is a very effective way to start new connections.

Do not forget to network within your company, too, especially if you are looking to climb up the ladder. In larger companies, there are many ways to connect with your coworkers: join interest groups who are working for a cause like supporting LGBT groups or the environment. Within these groups, you connect with colleagues you usually don't know. I also highly recommend that you ask a high-level executive to have lunch or a coffee with you. Most people seem very reticent about this, but the truth is: if people with decision-making power over your career do not know who you are and what you're doing in the company, the chances of you receiving that coveted promoted are slim.

Prioritize Networking.

Networking is like your new fitness regime. You will not see any benefits after one session. Like everything important in life, it requires an investment of time, perseverance, and commitment. Building new and authentic connections takes quality time. People with an extended portfolio of connections are people who have been actively networking for years. And I am not talking about followers on social media. I am talking about real connections. The investment in time and energy in building your network should become as important as the effort you are putting to cultivate your ambition.

Go Prepared.

Whatever your goal is, you need to do some background research before joining a group, an event or contacting someone digitally. This research implies looking up who the event organizer is, who will be speaking, and the company that this person is associated with. Many people underestimate background research and miss big opportunities. People who join the organizational committee or are leading some kind of group are themselves very well connected and very open to establishing new connections. Take the opportunity to connect with them. When contacting someone you don't know, it is good to tell the person why you would like to connect with them.

If you are building your network within your company, look up the management team, the people in the departments you would like to move into, and colleagues that you don't know. If you intend to progress in your company, knowing who is the decision-maker for the promotion you are aiming for is key.

You need to be prepared too. It is always good to have a business card ready. I also suggest having your professional digital profile ready (i.e., LinkedIn, Xing, or whatever other platforms you use). Make sure that your profile is well written as this is your 'digital first impression.' Get your elevator pitch ready! This includes who you are, what you do and what you are looking for and or what you are good at. Work on a good handshake (which I suppose is more applicable in the pre-COVID 19 world. Not sure what the current equivalent is).

Network!

At this stage, you have your networking strategy. If you are new in town and are looking for new connections, you may go to cooking classes and to networking events. If you are looking for a new job, you may start to connect digitally and during specific events. If you want to progress in your company, you may start to have lunches, coffee and face to face meetings with your colleagues and management.

A couple of pieces of advice here: if you decided to join networking events, don´t go with a friend and spend the whole event chatting to people you already know. Start conversations with people you don't know and spend a maximum of ten minutes with each person. In ten minutes, you will understand if this person is interesting or not. If you do find them interesting, schedule a one-to-one follow-up and take your time to connect better with that person. If they are not interesting, find a quick escape to the conversation and move on with the next connection.

If you are building your network within your organization, push yourself to connect with people in high management. It may take time to schedule something, but it is worth it.

In any case, if you feel that scheduling something with a person becomes difficult, read between the lines. Maybe they just don't want to connect with you. Don't be discouraged by this. There are plenty of people out there. Don't push yourself onto people.

Follow up.

At this stage, if you have followed my advice, you have met some new interesting people, and you have started to increase your network. After exchanging business cards (or after a lunch date with a colleague), and connecting via LinkedIn or other social media, it is time for a meaningful follow-up. Do not send those horrible standard messages, but personalize your invitation to connect over some elements you have shared during your conversation. Remember to be personal and authentic. I cannot repeat this enough. Networking is not about becoming friends or just looking for people to solve your problems. It is about creating a meaningful connection. Creating authentic connections will enable you to reach out to those people later in life, and those people may connect with you and ask for something too. In that case, if you have established a good relationship, you will be more inclined to help them, connect further or support them in their new projects. If the connection you have built is superficial and temporary, you will not be open to help them because you don't know their values, business ethic and real intentions.

I have given you a toolkit for starting your networking journey. You need to fill in the rest and find what works best for your personality, your family, and your work life. The global pandemic that we are all still living under has posed a particular challenge to networking. But we all need to adapt our strategies so that we can network effectively in a digital space. If you are an ambitious professional, I recommend you to set some simple goals to start, like connecting with one person you don't know once a week digitally and have lunch or coffee with someone that you don't know at least twice per month.

Find your tribe. Build a reliable network of people who help you at home. Have your close circle friend who deeply cares about you. Find a group of women who inspire you and where you can get ideas and support.

At work, build your working strategy and career wisely. Do not overwork yourself; be wise with your choice when it comes to career and family conflict. At work and home, delegate as much as possible and focus on the areas that makes you happy, and makes you move forward, and where your skills are demanded. And delegate ruthlessly everything else. Your time and energy are precious resources you need to manage as carefully as your money.

Most important: Ask for help! You cannot do it all alone!

CHAPTER FIVE

Don't Let Guilt Eat You

Valeria ran down the street towards her son's school. The performance had started at 17h, half an hour ago. **Why did these things have to start so early?** *For working parents to get to the school at this time of the afternoon meant leaving in the middle of the work day. She knew that the doors would not be open the whole evening, so she went as fast as she could. She climbed the stairs to the front entrance and ran right past the greeter. Her son was playing Hansel, in* **Hansel** and **Gretel** *performed by the first-grade class. She knew that it would be adorable, and she really did want to go but she couldn't help but feel guilty for leaving midway through a meeting that she had been working on for several weeks.* **Is missing the end of the meeting jeopardizing my reputation at work? Should I have stayed until the end?**

She felt like she was never able to give 100% to either her work or her children. **How can I ever get ahead at work if I need to leave so early? How will my son react to me being so late?** *Her husband was home with their daughter. The responsibility to watch and praise their son's achievement was on her.*

Valeria opened the large double doors to the school's auditorium where the play was underway. She briskly walked down the aisle to her seat. Thankfully, her son was not on the stage yet, they must have started later than planned. Not thinking much of it, she shrugged and got comfortable. Within minutes, her son emerged from backstage and sang his song with confidence. Valeria was so proud and even felt a few tears fall down her cheek. Valeria wasn't sure if these were tears brought on by extreme pride or by her guilt of thinking about work while she was sitting there watching her son perform. **Why do I always feel conflicted about my work and my family? Is there a way I can get rid of this constant feeling of guilt?**

A Personal Journey

There are two things in the world that make me feel guilty: my relationship with my mother and, and the outcome of my business Birdhaus. Both of these situations have a strong connection with my ambition.

The relationship with my mother is conflictual at its best and nonexistent at its worst.

It was not easy to grow up with someone like my mother. She was unstable, unpredictable, and without a consistent goal for her life. In my early teenage years, the roles reversed, and I took care of her until I left the house and started my adult life in Geneva. Years later, I concluded that her lack of professional ambition, consistency, and unconditional love motivated me to be the person and the mother I am now.

I didn't grow up surrounded by highly ambitious family or friends. In my childhood, people close to me were ordinary (mostly) and happily cruising in their life without major life goals besides a balanced existence. While in high school, I became friends with people who dreamed of becoming a world-recognized surgeon, Nobel Prize winners, or leading a political revolution. I mean, who does not dream big in high school? Despite these highly ambitious friends, my only goal was to finish high school, move to another city (and away from my mother) and start university.

It was at university where I began to learn that I need big goals too. Surrounded by scientists of all sorts, my education as a pharmacist showed me how much I liked to be put in front of scientific challenges and keep learning. There was a time when I wanted to pursue research (and why not aim for a Nobel Prize?). Still, after some time, I was convinced that the pharmaceutical industry world was in my future.

Three factors helped me start to think big:

My Corporate Career
Within the corporate culture, performance reviews, and internal politics, I felt like you really have two choices for your career path: thrive in your career and grow, or stay where you are.

-

Female Professional Networking
This was discussed in detail in chapter four, 'Find Your Tribe'.

-

My Relationship With My Husband
Having a healthy, ambitious man by my side who supports my goals with unconditional love is and has always been the key to my achievements.

Letting Go of the Guilt

In my late twenties, I started to really think about what my dreams and goals are for life and go after them. I felt confident doing this as I knew that I had a loving and supportive partner in my life. But this came with a cost. I needed to let go of my mother because her presence was a disrupting element, which would have never allowed me to live my life to the fullest. The guilt toward my failed relationship with her was heavy in the first years. Despite my rational decision, my emotions were not always aligned with my pragmatism. It took me years to achieve acceptance and, in the end, gratitude.

I had to grieve over my relationship with my mother as we do with a loss: going through all steps of grieving, sometimes moving one step forward and two backward, while dealing with my conflicting feelings and the guilt projected by other persons. Learning to be self-compassionate and forgive myself for the failed relationship took time and eased the omnipresent feeling of guilt.

Something that I have learned while I was dealing with this guilt was the importance of facing the root of the problem with immediacy. I realized that it was important for my mental health to deal with it instead of pushing it aside. Awareness can transform guilt into forgiveness, then from forgiveness into gratitude.

I'm a big fan of Sherly Sandberg's book *Option B*, which she wrote after she lost her husband. The book describes her journey with grief, and I was surprised at how much I connected with her while reading it. Even if my mother is still alive, and my coworking space closure is not as dramatic as losing someone, I was still experiencing a grief journey. Her words helped me to better understand the journey I'm on and deal with guilt, shame, and sadness in a more healthy way. She writes, *"Self-compassion comes from recognizing that our imperfections are part of being human. Those who can tap into [these concepts] can recover from hardship faster."* [51]

In my early twenties, I learned to be resilient without even knowing it. I took full control of my life, my goals, and my beliefs. I learned that my mother's choices and mistakes did not affect my whole life, and I chose to be surrounded by people who showed me unconditional love and friendship would help me go through everything.

BIRDHAUS AND COVID-19

With Birdhaus, the story is way more recent and related to my professional ambitions. When I bought Birdhaus, the founder was leaving the country and was looking for someone to take over a one-year-old women's coworking space social club in Zurich. It was a moment in my life where everything was running smoothly. My career in pharmaceuticals was not particularly challenging but still interesting. My leadership at the Professional Women's Group was established and without major problems. And my home life was organized and running well. Everything was looking up.

I had big dreams for Birdhaus. But of course I did. I calculated risks and pondered the investment. I surrounded myself with top professionals to help me develop the business. I had plenty of good ideas to implement and the energy to thrive. I quickly became the entrepreneur I didn't know I could be. In the middle of my new entrepreneurial journey, I focused full time on my business and left my corporate job's safety. But life is unpredictable. I mean, who knew that a global pandemic would crush all my plans within twelve months? COVID-19 took a toll on me, and like billions of people around the world, I could not have imagined that one day we were not going to able to leave our homes and meet other people for weeks. For a business based on people meeting each other in a physical space, sharing ideas, and having events, social distancing was a killer.

It was two days after I made the public announcement that Birdhaus would not open its doors again and all I could do was sit in its beautiful space, alone, crying. All kinds of emotions were there, and guilt was one of the strongest. The guilt of having dedicated way too many resources in a business without a future. The guilt of having prioritized my business over my family too often. Guilt to have exposed my family to a significant financial risk.

Somehow I did stay positive and pragmatic throughout the COVID-19 lockdown and the crisis, knowing very well that the circumstances played a massive role in my business destiny. I stayed active, shifted to virtual events, and connected with the members via newsletters and social media. There was not very much that I could have done differently to save it. I was surrounded by great advisors, who were especially present during the crisis.

Still, on that day, all the objective analysis and realistic considerations went to hell. I lost money, time, and energy in a space that was closing, and I felt impossibly guilty and sad. And worst of all, for the first time in a long time, I found myself without a plan for my professional life.

There's this quote that says, *"Entrepreneurs jump off a cliff and build parachutes on their way down."* [52] In my case, my cliff was about 2000 meters deep at the beginning of my jump. The global COVID-19 pandemic cut my cliff in half, and I crashed before taking advantage of the full height. Oops.

All alone in an empty space usually full of vibrant women hustling, I looked at my computer screen and tried to read all the messages I got from people after the closure announcement. There were messages of friendship and support mixed with disconcerting requests filling my inbox. My to-do list for the closure of the space was endless. I tried to focus, but it was impossible. My usual active and 'get things done' self was nowhere to be seen.

It did not take me long to understand that I could not recover from such a seismic shock alone. I always surround myself with the right people to help me with my goals. And my team was right there to support me: friends at work and at the NGO, my children's nanny, my family and my closest friends. But for this type of crash, I knew I needed more than just my regular team of support, so I called upon the help of a therapist and life coach and started my healing journey.

STARTING AGAIN
Thanks to my participation in sports, balanced nutrition, daily meditation, and self-development exercises, I understood the root cause of my guilt. My ambition led me to buy Birdhaus, and my drive pushed me to overwork myself in all parts of my life for over a year. COVID-19 put me

in a situation I could not control any longer. I needed to get over my guilt to be able to start new. While working on my new life plan and finding balance again, the world kept suffering from the COVID-19 outbreak. I quickly realized how my circumstances, my family support and the Swiss system softened my blow. Millions of people lost their loved ones, their jobs, and or their businesses without having a solid support system in place. The OECD (Organization for Economic Cooperation and Development) report noted:

"The COVID-19 pandemic has triggered one of the worst jobs crises since the Great Depression. There is a real danger that the crisis will increase poverty and widen inequalities, with the impact felt for years to come (OECD, 2020)." [53]

This awareness helped me to speed up my recovery and embrace gratitude.

In a moment suspended in time, with a glass of wine in my hand looking into the evening sky, I told myself that I should put my striving and ambition aside. I should take a step back from my mission to contribute to gender equality for a little while and accept any kind of job and cruise in a peaceful life for a couple of years. This thought remained in my head for a couple of days until I shook it off. I'm not that type of person. And I'm not someone who settles for anything. I want more and better things for myself and my family. I want to move forward with my life, and I want to contribute to achieving gender quality, no matter what.

My professional life was suspended, my business reframed in digital service, my contribution to a more gender-balanced world inexistent. To the world, I was jobless, and my entrepreneurial life finished. But I'm more than my job title or my business financial statement. Even without a defined professional goal (yet), I remain an ambitious and driven person who wants to contribute to a cause. I just needed to find my new way and keep going.

Awareness can transform guilt into forgiveness, then from forgiveness into gratitude.

And if there is a message you need to take out of this book, it is this one: being an ambitious person cannot be switched off. Sure, some circumstances will put you in a very hard situation like divorce, job loss, relocation, health issues. There are challenges along the road, and it is not easy to be an ambitious working parent today. But we can build resilience and keep going with a growth mindset.

We need to allow ourselves to take a break, rest, and ask for help. Bounce back, aim for more and better and keep aligned with your goals. But most important: remain true to yourself.

When I started to write this book, the COVID-19 pandemic was simmering in the background in China. My life plans were very different from what they are now. The idea I had about this chapter was different. In fact, this chapter stumped my writing journey for months as I was on the path to healing. In my time of need, I reached out to other mothers who had grown children and who were no longer experiencing the guilt of dedicating so much of yourself to something other than your small children. I wanted them to look back and tell me what it was like for them and inform my healing journey. And that is exactly what they did for me.

LOOKING BACK
Being a working mother is a hell of a job, and you face challenges all the time. Guilt seems like a companion who will be close to you the entire way. Your plan will change because of circumstances you cannot control. The only thing you can control is how you react to what hits you and do your best to keep going.

There are so many different types of guilt that can come up in a working mother's life. There will be days where your kids drive you insane, and your only solace is a glass of red wine on the balcony after they go to sleep. Guilt will come up because, for an awful moment, you wanted to lock the kids in their rooms and throw away the key, but of course, you wouldn't. But nonetheless, you feel guilty about a thought; this is a mom's life.

There are days you will have to turn down a business meeting to go to your child's school activity. You go to your child's activity feeling guilty that you missed a great opportunity that could have boosted your career. And in the same way, you know that you would feel guilty if you did not go to your child's school activity.

Sometimes, people make you feel guilty by what they say to you in the grocery store or even as you pass by on the street. This type of guilt is a projection of someone else's' expectations for you and your family. Or even worse, there is the guilt that will inevitably come when your child gets old enough to tell you how you are missing the mark. This type of guilt is strong enough to make you rethink your whole life and ask yourself if all your effort is worth it.

Unfortunately, there is no set guideline to follow in order to get rid of your guilt. But this is the advice that I will give you; all working mothers have felt guilt and struggled with it. It is important to stay true to ourselves, embrace who we are, keep wanting more and better for ourselves and our families.

DEFINITION

Looking into the meaning of the word guilt, we understand it is a big word. According to the *Collins Dictionary* guilt is *"... an unhappy feeling that you have because you have done something wrong or think that you have done something wrong."*[54]

While writing this book, I asked several mothers what their meaning of guilt is.

Most women told me that guilt is a bad feeling that will grab your guts during your whole life as a parent. Once during an event a woman told me: *"If I want to meet a mother who overcame guilt, look for someone older, whose children are now adults. [Look for] someone who has wisdom and who found peace and is ok with all that she did."*

This comment made me think and rethink. Is that true? We will find our inner peace and be guilt-free only when our kids are old, and we are enjoying retirement? Looking around me, I notice that this feeling is universal and that it has only increased during the COVID-19 lockdown. COVID-19 forced us all to be in the same house day after day. It forced us to think about our priorities in life. While taking care of the children, we feel guilty that we are not focusing enough on work. While working, we felt guilty not to dedicate enough time to our children. Not surprisingly, most parents were looking at their childless friends with envy.

Guilt is related to the act of doing something wrong, and while listening to all the mothers around me, I started to think this is a feeling imprinted in our DNA. No one can escape it. But is that true? Are we really doing something wrong? And against who or what?

SHIFTING THE VIEW

Everyone thinks about our guilt toward family, but what about our guilt towards our professional life? A missed career opportunity because of the idea that the kids need their mother at home more than in the working world will negatively impact a woman sooner or later (especially the professionally ambitious ones). However, this guilt is going to be a different one and will grow with time. It will start with frustration that will spill out in an argument with your partner and then with your child. Later it will come when a friend gets that great job. Yes, I mean THAT job! And in a nasty moment of complete and utter frustration, you will think, "I dedicated my whole life to our family and threw away my career for you!" I will let you complete the rest of this story.

I have heard this nasty thought a couple of times in my life from friends who were in the middle of a divorce or who had to deal with turbulent teenagers. Now don't hear what I am not saying. I don't mean that every woman who dedicates her life to her family is secretly frustrated. But I am saying that this is sometimes the case and that it is important to raise awareness of this fact. In our society's background, there is an underestimated sentiment of all these brilliant and capable professional women who have decided the feelings of regret, guilt and shame to leave their little children in child care were too high to bear. So they traded their current guilt of not seeing their children with the potential future guilt of missing professional opportunities.

Giving up on dreams and professional ambitions will have, in the long run, the same result of missing time with your family. In the publication, *The Experience of Regret: What, When, and Why,* by Thomas Gilovich and Victoria Husted Medvec, findings indicate that "*...there is a temporal pattern to the experience of regret. Actions, or errors of commission, generate more regret in the short term; but inactions, or errors of omission, produce more regret in the long run.*"[55] In simple words, over time, people tend to regret the chances they missed and not the mistakes they made. "*When people look back in their lives, it seems to be their regrettable failures to act that stand out and causes greater grief.*" (In addition to that, there was no evidence that showed older children were impacted by their time in childcare during their early years. This is most likely because they don't even remember their early years.

Are society expectations the main drive of mother's guilt? I would suggest that maybe they are. Sure enough, to be a good parent today is not an easy task.

As we all know, the list that accompanies the job of a mother is endless. We all want to ensure that the children eat well, get exercise, have friends, and are well mannered. We want to teach them to be independent and develop their own thoughts and feelings. We hope that in the end, the result is this perfect kid who is happy, healthy, empathic, strong, responsible, creative, sporty, musician, and able to choose a local product to support the local farmers.

Now all I have to say to this is, no wonder we as mothers carry around so much guilt. The milestones are sky high, and let's face it; there really isn't enough time in a lifetime to meet those goals. So why not decide that the best we can do is enough? By the way, it is important to note that I've never spoken to a father who has all of these expectations for his parenting. I always said, my husband and I are the judges of the well-being and happiness of our children. If they don't go to the afterschool ballet, football, swimming classes, piano, and chess class and they don't rescue an animal in distress in their spare time, that is perfectly fine with us.

Glimpses into the World of Mother Guilt

The following fragments are part of working mother interviews I collected over the years for my blog and for this book. Some of them are published in my blog, and some are part of the focus group. The topic of guilt is so sensible and personal. All these stories are anonymous to preserve the mothers' privacy.

O. ARTIST IN HER THIRTIES WITH ONE CHILD.

Sometimes, I suffer from my husband's ambition. My husband projects his professional ambition and life expectations on my work, and he became restless. I push myself to finish my projects, move forward, but all the while, I am thinking I'm not doing enough, that I'm not ambitious enough. I have my objectives, but I always want to follow my pace, and this sometimes does not correspond with his. Then I feel guilty because I start to think that I'm not pushing my projects quickly enough or that I'm neglecting important tasks related to work because I need to take care of my child. Sometimes I'm just confused about where to set priorities. But when I shut down what he says and guide him through my way of thinking, we are fine again. He understands, and I don't feel guilty anymore.

R. ENTREPRENEUR AND SINGLE MOM OF THREE.

Shortly after arriving back to Switzerland, as a single mom with three children, from living in India and Bali for a few years, I realized how important it was for us all to have a supportive partner and father. Of course I wanted to keep going with my coaching business in Switzerland too. But only a few weeks later, I already felt so exhausted physically, mentally and emotionally from coping with, arranging and carrying everything on my own. At one point I didn't even have the energy to prepare breakfast for my children, so I had to give them into my parents' care. And I couldn't live my soul's purpose by sharing my gift with humanity in this condition. I felt so guilty, depressed, weak, lonely and fearful. To keep up with a balance between caring for the children, household, and trying to maintain a healthy lifestyle while earning money, was impossible. I needed help but the father of the kids neither supported me financially nor cared for the kids. Deep fears of scarcity were building up in my whole system. At my deepest point of depression and weakness, I realized I had to take deep inhalations to bring my life force energy back, get up and embody again what I was teaching the world: "I'm here to infuse more juice and passion to your life." And so I did!

D. ENTREPRENEUR IN HER FIFTIES WITH TWO CHILDREN.

I'm a strong advocate of feminism, but I don't think that all women have to be dedicated in the same fashion to this cause. Every woman has to make her own decisions, based on herself and her family's needs. Not every woman wants to keep working once children arrive on the scene, and we have to accept that. There are not good or bad decisions when it comes to the family to business equilibrium. The most important thing is to make conscious decisions as mothers and fathers and to be happy with those.

C. CORPORATE PROFESSIONAL IN HER FIFTIES WITH ONE CHILD.

Guilt evolves and diminishes with time. I'm a single working mother with high career ambition, and I make it work for my daughter and for me. When she was a baby and toddler, I cried every day after dropping her off at the daycare, and once again, when I picked her back up at the end of the day. But when I was at the office, I was happy. When I decided to relocate and put distance between my daughter and her family, everyone told me I was "pulling out the roots of this poor child." Both grandmothers were taking turns, making me feel guilty. I'll let you imagine how that felt. I knew this was the best decision for her and for me.

With time it became the challenge of my life to show that I could have an accomplished career and raise my child alone. There have been times that I became overwhelmed by the pressure to be an involved and caring mother, my demanding job making me work during the night, and having to cope with challenges alone.

Sometimes I have been labeled a Superwoman because I was thriving at work during the week and going with my daughter and her girlfriend for a ski day on the weekend. I did that because I felt guilty I could not spend more time with her during the week. But people saw it as something an overachieving mother would do. With time I realized that I needed to prioritize myself, learn to say no, and always be honest with my daughter. Kids understand more, and so we need to share where we stand and how we feel. Now, years later, I can sit back and watch her be a young, grounded and intelligent woman ready to conquer the world, and I know all my efforts have been worth it.

K. AN ENTREPRENEUR IN HER THIRTIES WITH TWO CHILDREN.

I feel guilty when I cannot take care of everything by myself at home and in my business. My natural inclination is to solve all problems when they show up. Soon I realized that I could not possibly do it all by myself. So I learned to delegate, both at home at in my business. It took me a while to get to this mindset, and sometimes I fell back into this habit of doing it all.

I felt guilty about my business when I could not dedicate enough time to it because of my family, and I felt guilty with my family when my business took all my energy away. The worst of all of this was that I could not enjoy time with them while feeling guilty. In hindsight, I can say that I'm happy with my life choices. I have a business I love, a wonderful family, great friends, and for a little while, I finally get to cut out some time for me.

N. ENTREPRENEUR IN HER FORTIES WITH THREE CHILDREN.

Last year was an intense year for my business, and I did not find enough time for me or for my husband. But the business was running, and I had to keep going. And I loved my job because it is my passion, so I don't feel like my job is an obligation. My kids now know I'm very busy. I'm their mom in the evening and during the weekend. I'm raising them to be independent and to do their stuff alone as well. But without an au-pair or nanny, it is very difficult. I'm not that flexible. The Swiss childcare and school system do not help working moms like me. Despite all of the system's weaknesses, it is enormously expensive! Anyway, I'm determined to make it work, so I have found my own solutions.

A. ENTREPRENEUR IN HER THIRTIES WITH TWO CHILDREN.

Guilt is like a bad smell that sticks with you for a long time but at one point it disappears.

When I decided to move to a new city to follow my boyfriend, I didn't speak a word of the local language and I didn't have a job. Two weeks after I moved, the 2008 financial crisis hit and it was much harder to find a job. I felt guilty, as after only six months of relationship, this wonderful man was now supporting me with everything.

Then a few years later, when I became a mom and decided to work 60% of the time, I felt guilty to put my career aside. I was very ambitious regarding my career and seeing my responsibilities drop because of my part-time work was a real challenge. In the end, working part-time sounded like a good deal but I felt guilty not to be happy in this situation. I was struggling between being an ambitious professional or a 'good' mom. It took me a few years to understand that being a 'good' mom was not about spending all my time with my kids but spending quality time with them full of love and good intentions.

Today, my guilt has disappeared because I have done some deep self-reflections. I had to reflect why I felt so guilty during all those years when my husband was supporting me. I had to reflect on why I felt so guilty not to be the perfect businesswoman, the perfect wife and the perfect mom. I think when you start to find the answers and become aligned with yourself, your guilt starts to disappear like this bad smell which used to stick around.

B. CORPORATE CAREER, IN HER FIFTIES WITH ONE CHILD.

It is easy to feel guilty when we are in a society that expects us to be a super mama. In order not to be get weighed down by this, you have to listen primarily to your inner voice and take comments from your family, friends or society with a little bit of distance. For some women, the inner voice will tell you to focus on her children; for others, like me, it can be different. Be aware that we are living in a new social paradigm. When in human history, have women ever had the time and freedom to say, "I will take care of my child full time?" I believe that a lot of today's guilty feelings are related to societal pressure.

CHAPTER SIX

Cultivate a Growth Mindset

The moment had finally come. A position was open in the digital marketing department. Valeria would be able to pursue her ambition of being more involved in the creative side of her marketing firm. Although this was what she wanted to do, she was afraid of applying for the position. She sat in her seat on the train, thinking long and hard about her options. She could stay in the position she was in, which held no promises for promotion or further development, but was beneficial for her family balance, because it was flexible and not too demanding. She knew she was essentially just 'cruising' in her professional life. **Do I want to keep doing this? It's the easiest and smartest thing to do, right?** *she thought to herself.* **Or do I want to learn new things and challenge myself? Do I want something more and better?** *She honestly was not sure if she had the right skillset for the position. When she was younger, and had more time, she had fancied herself an artist, drawing nature scenes and portraits and exploring new way of expression. But she hadn't done that in years.* **Why did I stop?** *Ah, yes, lack of time. The more she thought of this new opportunity, the more afraid she was.* **What if I completely fail and then they don't give me my other job back? Why if it is too stressful and my family suffer?** *There were definitely risks involved. But then the other half of her thought,* **What if I am actually really good at this and enjoy my work more? What if this position offers me new and better opportunities in the company? What if I become the next head of design or have the opportunity to create my own department? What if I could enroll in an art school and develop my creative side?** *Her heart fluttered in her chest, thinking about the wonderful opportunities that awaited her if she applied. Valeria took another look at her life and realized that she hadn't taken a risk in years. And thus far, her ambitions at work had been frozen to give priority to her family needs. She was not able to take advantage of the opportunities for development in the ways that she had hoped to. Maybe this was her opportunity.* **Maybe I should trust that my family can handle some organizational changes and allow me to thrive at work. Maybe I need to change how I am thinking about myself and be more open to new things and developing new skills. And if I fail then... there are plenty of marketing jobs I suppose.**

Valeria decided that she would do it. She was going to apply for the design position!

Interview with Amanda Lamb

Sometimes the universe shows you a way to meet amazing people, and you just have to follow that path.

Thanks to my blog and my quest to interview working mothers around the world, I got the chance to find Amanda Lamb's website. Never in a million years did I think that we would have had the chance to talk. She is a TV reporter, working mom, blogger, book writer and half-marathon runner from North Carolina in the United States. When I found her website, I was very impressed and slightly intimidated. She is a woman of one thousand activities, a television personality, and a very well-established writer with nine published books. I hesitated for a couple of days before contacting her for my project, *Meet Another Working Mom (Ana Just Ana,* 2019). Finally, I was courageous enough to send her a message. Then it would seem that some magic happened! She replied and found time for me within a couple of days in her very busy schedule.

We start talking about her life as a writer. She wrote her first book ages ago and, very much like me, the piece was stored safely for a long time in a drawer (yep, at that time there was not a computer folder...). The memoir was about her life as a mother and as a wife. After a careful search, she found an agent in California who believed in her, and she published her first book *Smotherhood* in 2007.[56] From then on, Amanda wrote crime books, mostly based on real crime cases she followed as a reporter and more memoirs. In the meantime, she keeps her followers posted about the latest parenting news in her blog – *Go and Ask Mom* – while working full time as a reporter.

I had been speaking with her for fifteen minutes, and I was very impressed. Her's was more than a busy life. How did she manage? Is there time for relaxation in her life?

Amanda: *"Everyone has a different Zen,"* – she tells me with a big smile – *"I like to run, for example, and this gives me energy. While running, I listen to podcasts because I still want to do something useful. I keep busy, and I like to be surrounded by people who have a lot going on."*

Yes, this I can fully understand – in fact, this sounds very much like me.

Every one of us has a role model that we can follow – a woman to look at and admire, someone who can teach us the fundamentals of life. For Amanda, this person was her mother. When her mother was diagnosed with cancer, she took her home and spent the last weeks of her life taking care of her. This is a very poignant story that Amanda shared with the public via her blog and then in her book.

Amanda: *"I took a family leave for my mother. When I started to share our journey, I realized that I had lots of followers coming from my TV work. People started to see me as a normal human being and not like the serious reporter they were used to knowing. I discovered that writing, while my mom was ill, was important not only for me but for my followers as well."*

Her mother never read her blog, but she was aware of it and listened to the followers' comments when Amanda was reading it. Watching Amanda speaking about her mother, I saw a lot of emotions surfacing, and the most evident of those was pride.

> Amanda: *"My mother was a lawyer in the '70s. She was a force of nature who did everything because back then, she did not have a choice. She taught me that it is very important to have something that is only yours, a project not related to anyone else other than you. She also supported me to continue to work when my daughter got a severe case of meningitis as a baby. I wanted to leave everything to stay with her. My mother always told me that I could continue to work, but it is not going to be easy."*

And here I'm facing a grateful daughter praising her working mother. Amanda continues to tell me how important her mother was as a role model for her and how, now, she feels the responsibility to do the same for her two daughters.

> Amanda: *"I want my daughters to know that I'm going to be in the wings to support and cheer for them, no matter what they do. I'm raising them to be independent and capable of achieving whatever they want."* [57]

Now that her children have grown, Amanda is thinking about the future and her next steps. She is excited to know what is going to happen when her nest is empty and how she and her husband will reframe their life. Of course, she is not waiting quietly. Recently, she started a communications consulting business to help people improve their public speaking, and she is writing two books – one for children and one adult fiction novel. Of course, she is doing all of this while keeping up her work for the TV network and running half-marathons (check out her social media pages. They are very inspiring!).

I would have liked to continue our conversation, but it was past midnight in Zurich, and suddenly, my baby girl woke up, waking up her big brother, and my husband. My interesting conversation about the current book market situation was interrupted by the well-rehearsed concert of my children screaming! My time with Amanda was over.

I remember leaving my laptop with the feeling that I could have talked to Amanda for at least another two hours, and I could have asked her so much more! I would have loved to learn how to become a good writer like her. I would have loved to probe her for some tips on how to manage it all as a working mother and somehow find Zen at the same time. I guess we will have to save that for another midnight call.

I contacted Amanda before publishing this book again. Since the time we talked on that late night in fall 2019, she finished a children's book, a novel, launched a podcast and was writing another novel.

Where Curiosity Leads

I have always been a curious person. I often joke that if someone made a compelling case, I would start to collect and study butterflies. I am known to be an avid reader and someone open to listening to and supporting the craziest stories and initiatives without judgment. Still, I would never guess that as a pharmacist, I would one day publish a romance novel, lead a female nonprofit organization and buy a women's only coworking space. Looking back, my curiosity was my starting point to cultivate my growth mindset. A mindset where we see the world full of opportunities, and every challenge is a chance to learn something new. When I spoke with people like Amanda Lamb, I loved to feel their sparkle and their enthusiasm. These kinds of people start new adventures and put the same effort and commitment to their new project like it was their job.

Earlier in the book, I pointed out how important it is to surround yourself with the right people. It goes without saying that if the people around you have interesting personalities and challenge themselves with new projects, ideas, and professional goals, you will most probably follow the same example. Talking about other people's projects and challenges will develop your mind to: at first help them find a solution, and think about what you could do too.

Cultivating a growth mindset is critical for ambitious people: we cannot achieve great objectives by remaining the way we are. Ambition runs in parallel to professional development and personal growth. It should be a lifestyle embedded in our everyday routine. Technology today allows us to be continuously connected to new learning opportunities. So let's use this time and technology in the right way and cut the consumption of useless social media content and trash videos. In fact, it was only thanks to technology that I was able to become a writer and a blogger. I discovered that if writing is not my strength, storytelling is, and apparently, you can do a lot with that.

I'M NOT A GOOD WRITER,
YET I'M A BLOGGER AND PUBLISHED AUTHOR

Curiosity and learning can lead to very unexpected paths. For instance, I never thought I'd publish a novel – *NEXT 9* – let alone tell the tale of how I wrote it. And yet, here I am to tell you how I turned a word file into a book.

I'd like to preface this by saying that, back in high school, my teachers in Italian, other languages, and history would often frown over my essays, then at me, and say that really, REALLY, I wasn't a gifted writer, which is partly why I chose to study science at university. I've always known I wasn't much of a writer and, if you ask my friends or my husband, they'll confirm it. So why on earth did I decide to write and publish a novel?

Well, it all happened a bit by chance. During my first pregnancy, my gynecologist ordered me to stay home and rest from the fifth month on. For an active person like me, it was pretty much like condemning me to one of the circles of hell. After reading a large number of books and realizing that I couldn't stand television (so no, Netflix was not an option!), I decided it was time to find another outlet for my energy that would still allow me to sit on the couch. That's how I started to write a little story. Meanwhile, I got plenty of visits from my friends, most of them single, who told me tales of bad dates, breakups and the trials of being single in the city. *"One day, I'll write a book about your dramas!"* I always joked. And here was the perfect opportunity. I started writing about the stories of people in search of love to pass the time.

Then I stopped. I read over the first pages and found them horrible. I started searching the web for ways to improve my writing and found a myriad of sites to help a budding writer.

Then one day, I read an article that turned my hesitation into determination: it said that the only way to learn to write better was to write more. My narrative project continued with focused research and drew inspiration from books and films. I wrote until the birth of my son. I finished the story while I was on maternity leave and filed it away on my MacBook for over a year (I called it *Project Two*).

Back at work on my lunch break, I told a friend about it, and, as an avid reader of novels, she asked me to send her the file. She was curious to read it. Hesitantly, I sent her the text. She sent it back to me full of corrections but convinced that it was a good story. I then sent it to another friend for a second opinion and further corrections. He read the file, corrected it and told me to keep going. By then, I was at a crossroads. I didn't have much faith in my project, but why not give it a try?

The road to publishing has been long. It took me more than two years from the moment I finished the *NEXT 9* manuscript to its release date in November 2018.[58] I've learned so much in the process that pushed me not only to do it all over again but also to help other women to do the same. Thanks to Birdhaus coworking space, I enjoyed meeting many other writers and aspiring writers. Listening to their struggle as authors and to the questions they had about writing, publishing and promoting their books; I started to share my experience and connect them to the right professionals. I ended up creating a dedicated group for women authors called 'Birdhaus Writers' and a tailored writing and publishing event program. While Birdhaus coworking space closed its physicals doors in May 2020, Birdhaus Writing & Publishing kept going. And, to this day, I still support women to write and publish their books.

So, if you're like me and you want to try something new, like publishing a book, I would encourage you to try it even if you think you're not very good at writing. Don't take people's word for it that you're not good at something. Just try it!

Here are some things that I've learned:

Writing is the easy bit.

Everything that comes after is incredibly hard. It doesn't matter if you are writing fiction or a nonfiction book; writing is the easiest (and most fun) part. Editing is a painful but necessary process. For both my books, I had to delete several passages, rewrite others, and still get feedback from my editors that "It is still not right." Then came the search within the publishing industry, the choice of which publishing format, of a literary agent (or not), the cover design and book layout, the translation (for my novel) and marketing. In the end, I invested less time in creating the narrative than I did in anything else. Thanks to the things that I learned while writing and publishing my first novel, the process with this book is more structured and less stressful.

Publishing a book is not a solo effort.

Like any other successful project, you need a strategy, a team, and well-coordinated execution. The picture of a writer looking dreamily into the horizon with a glass of wine and writing and publishing his masterpiece by himself is fiction. If writing can be done in the solitude of your home office (or balcony), publication cannot. The publication is a complex process, with lots of different phases to go through. It does not matter if you choose to self-publish or work with an agent and publishing house; you will need to invest a considerable number of resources in your book. No one is an expert at everything; finding the right people to help you with publishing and promoting a book is key.

Even though your friend's help is important, nothing compares to a professional opinion. I was certain I had written something of little interest, which is why my novel *NEXT 9* stayed put on my computer for over a year. It was only thanks to my Italian editor Barbara, and her experience in the publishing industry that I understood that I had a chance. Thanks to her expertise, I have learned what to expect when publishing my first novel. But choosing the right professionals wasn't without its share of difficulties. The web is full of promises of a good job done quickly and cheaply. I made some mistakes at the beginning of my publishing journey. I wish someone would have guided me at that time. This is one of the main reasons why I'm helping other women go through their book publishing process.

Create
a personal brand.

The concept of a personal brand is a trending topic in the last few years, and had it not been for my novel, I would never have grasped the true meaning. During the publishing process, someone told me: *"Ana, you're invisible online. If you want anyone to read your book outside of your circle of friends, you need to build yourself an image on social media and promote your work."* Thanks to that frank assessment of my online presence (or rather, my absence), I started working on my own personal brand. I launched my blog anajustana.com and started to use social media constructively (this still has room for improvement). In the last few years, I discovered that many new authors neglect the importance of building a personal brand and online presence BEFORE publishing their books. How will people find your book if you cannot be found anywhere?

Don't take yourself too seriously, but do believe in yourself.

I always knew I wasn't working on the next great novel, and I never for a minute thought I would be the next J. K. Rowling. I didn't believe in my work or myself as a writer. And that was a huge mistake because it just delayed the whole process of publishing my novel. The novel was always a low-priority project in my otherwise busy life. But at a certain point, I had to believe in it. After I published my first novel, I discovered how many people have the dream of 'writing a book'. So many people confessed their dream of wanting to write a book but do not even manage to finish their manuscript. This knowledge made me feel very proud of my achievement. After all, I did publish a novel, and becoming a writer has never even been a dream of mine.

Despite the glowing pride which comes from this achievement, I'm still very realistic. I don't think I will get rich and famous from my books. I believe that I have a message to share, and someone in the world needs to read it to move forward with her life.

It's the journey that matters.

I would advise everyone to write a book and publish it. What I learned from my books is invaluable. It's been such an important personal journey. My novel *Next 9* has helped me discover my love of writing, the accomplishment and pride of my first book published, and the importance of having a personal brand. This book, **Ambition Factor**, has helped me to create the first Birdhaus Writers Group. It supported me in my journey of healing and ultimately helped me to find a new version of myself.

SIDE-HUSTLES

Throughout the years, I have discovered that people with an open mind are the ones who experienced the most exciting situations in life. Many mothers I interviewed had side-hustles, which made them the most exciting people to hang around. While orchestrating the Birdhaus Writing and Publishing group, I meet many women writers (I have a fetish for writers, I can't help it) with day jobs that didn't stop them from having ambitions to write and publish their books. Some women had high-level corporate positions during the day and in the evenings would run their side-hustles in things like culinary events or photography.

Besides all being driven professionals and good mothers, they all had a crucial element in common: they invested in themselves. And by investing, I mean, they were always learning new skills and building their side-hustle. These women were taking photography courses, coding boot camp, public speaking classes or going to a writing academy. Every new skill that helped them cultivate their ambitions within and outside their working life brought with it fun, joy and success.

LEARNING THROUGH FAILURE

I've had several side-hustles myself. As you know, I had developed my women-only coworking space business called Birdhaus, which has now transitioned to being a virtual space due to the pandemic.

Years before I bought Birdhaus, I attempted a previous business startup. It took me about a month to develop a business plan, and I worked with two knowledgeable business-minded people to get the idea launched. But it was still a failed attempt. I won't bore you over the details, the point is that what is important about that experience is what I learned from it. I was able to take what I learned and apply it to Birdhaus business model years later. Through failure, I discovered my entrepreneurial spirit, values like respect and business ethics, and the importance of having like-minded people at your side while doing business.

In this way, I do not associate success with monetary value, the number of followers or even the relative popularity of my startup. I have come to understand that success in any venture, and especially a startup, is when you can come away having felt like your life has been enriched by the experience. I had fun and was challenged by sitting with business-minded people and developing my ideas with them. It was exciting to take a risk and think big, not knowing what could happen or how my idea would turn out.

So I would encourage you to take the successes and the failures together and not be discouraged.

We don't know where our curiosity will lead us. Be open-minded and follow some new path. Be creative and say yes to some unusual proposal. This attitude could probably lead you to some bad experiences, but every experience in life is a learning experience.

Interview with Mara Harvey

I first met Mara Harvey at the Lean In conference in Zurich in January 2019. She was one of the keynote speakers of a very inspiring conference. Her topic, however, was not only an inspiring story, but rather a wake-up call for all of us – 'When a pay gap leads you down an unexpected path'. The gender pay gap begins early – way earlier than we thought. It starts with pocket money. Myself, as many other women in the audience, were stupefied. How can it be that the parents are the first ones who are creating the gender pay gap?

Mara Harvey has published a series of four children's books: *A Smart Way to Start,* which are books that are helpful for exploring financial confidence for children in a very simple way. The stories explain important notions of working and earning money, equal pay, financial confidence, and sustainability. The books are a parent-child guide around one of the most crucial topics in life, and which is often kept as a taboo in many families: money.

I asked my first burning question: why did a wealth manager working in a big bank decide to write children books?

In her nineteen years of corporate experience, Mara has always been very engaged in gender equality, and she actively supported initiatives to give women the inspiration to grow professionally during her career. A decade ago, her professional path led her to take on a human resources position where she saw first-hand the gender gaps and lack of diversity in the financial world.

Mara: *"The lack of cultural diversity inside a company also reflects the lack of diversity while dealing with its clients," she says, referring to the fact the male dominated financial word could do better to understand their female clients, currently underserved. There is a lot more work to be done and a broad opportunity to be grasped."*

In 2018 Mara published *Women and Risk,* and while researching for this essay in 2017, she discovered that the gender pay gap starts with pocket money.[59]

One day in January of 2018, while watching a live stream from the Equality Lounge in Davos, by Shelley Zalis, CEO of The Female Quotient, Mara had her "Aha!!" moment: confidence starts at the age of five, and so does financial confidence.

Mara: *"I understood in that moment that if we want to have a conversation about gender pay gaps and gender equality in general, we need to start discussing it with our children at a very early age."*

Inspired and motivated by that, she decided to write a children's book explaining the notion of equal pay and financial confidence. Being a mother of two, she knew that the book needed to be interesting for the parents, because at the end of the day, who is buying and reading the book to our children? Exactly – it's us, the parents.

While Mara described the moment she started to write and the flow she was in, I recognized the energy and sparkle of a woman not only with a side hustle, but with a mission.

Mara: *"I knew what I wanted to say, I knew what the problems were, and I knew how to solve them."*

After her first version was born, she gave it to her 12-year-old daughter. To Mara's surprise, her daughter said, *"Mum, I don't speak bank"* and then *"Mum, I really don't see the problem: why would a girl earn less?"*

The first comment was easier to acknowledge and to fix: she needed to simplify the script. The second one, however, was way more profound.

Mara: *"We all seem to be unaware of the problem. If our girls don't see the problem, they wouldn't ask for their rights. And boys need to know that it is not okay to be paid more only because they are boys. The responsibility to raise conscious children is on us – the parents."*

Mara's words are crystal clear and make my mind go into full speed.

Thinking of my little girl, I ask myself if when she is thirty years old, will she still discuss gender equality with her friends? Will she still need to be engaged and fight for women's rights, or will she see this as an obsolete topic? Will she enter the workforce confident that the way her employer will treat her is the same as her brother?

I realize that raising our children into becoming conscious global citizens is one of the keys for a world of equality. Every parent should have gender equality very high in their education agenda, as much as well-behaved, well-nourished and environmentally conscious children.

Continuing our discussion, Mara tells me the future steps for her books. She wants to explore all dimensions around money and ethics for children, and her mission is to do it in a playful way.

Mara: *"Not only do I care about financial confidence in children, I strongly believe we need to teach our kids to spend their money consciously. The concepts of saving, investing and donating money are very important. Since money habits are shaped at the age of seven, we need to talk about those concepts very early in life."*

Before finishing our interview, Mara gave my little girl a lovely gift: a piggy bank! And not a random one, but a very conscious and lovely concept from Kinder-Cash. This special piggy bank has four compartments: spend, save, invest, donate. With this lovely present she reminds me:

Mara: *"Because money is not just a transmission of value, it's a transmission of values."*

This interview was the start of a great friendship. Mara joined the Birdhaus Advisory board and was at my side during the highs and the lows. Her banking career is thriving as well as her side hustle activities as a children's book writer. She is a wonderful example of a working mother with the **Ambition Factor.**

What's a Growth Mindset?

In the book *Mindset: The New Psychology of Success*, Carol Dweck illustrates how the world can be divided into two groups of people: those with a fixed mindset and those with a growth mindset.[60]

People with a fixed mindset accept the idea of predetermined abilities and talents. They think their skills cannot improve as they are fixed and permanent. People with a growth mindset believe that aptitude and skills are not fixed but can be learned and changed. According to Dweck, these mindsets lead to very distinctive behavior traits. For instance, people with fixed mindsets avoid new challenges and are usually quick to give up when they fail. They also tend to have a blaming attitude and try to find excuses and instead of a solution for their obstacles. People with a growth mindset are resilient, tenacious and view criticism and failure as part of the learning process.

In her book, Dweck provides many examples of both mindsets and how to recognize when we have a fixed mindset. The book is a great guide on how to change your beliefs and improve your life as a person, professional and especially as a parent.

In Fall 2019, I participated in a Forbes Women Summit DACH in Zurich. One of the main speakers, Janina Kugel, former Member of the Managing Board and Chief Human Resources Officer at Siemens, asked the audience how many hours a week we dedicate to learning something new. She gave the audience the answer to her question: Less than two hours, two to five hours, more than five hours.

She told the audience that, ideally, we should all be in the third group and dedicate more than five hours a week to develop and challenge ourselves.

The more we age, she added, the more time we should dedicate to learn new skills. I found this exercise fascinating, and I'm sure many people in the room had the same *Aha!* moment.

BACK TO THE PROBLEM OF TIME

For the ambitious working parents reading this book, your first thought might be, *"When can I find time to dedicate to learning new skills?"* And of course, I get it. Every mother gets it. It is hard to find time for yourself. Some days it is just too hard to focus, or we are just too tired to read before going to sleep, too irritated to think about learning, and too stressed out to actively keep a growth mindset. We tell ourselves as mothers that there is no time, but part of the truth here is that we do not prioritize time for ourselves.

Laura Vanderkam, an expert on time management and author of several productivity books, tells us the truth in regards to time management in her TedX *How to gain control of your free time.* She states that *"Time is highly elastic. We cannot make more time. The key to time management is treating our priorities like [an emergency]."*[61]

So just like maintaining a healthy diet, finding time to learn new things throughout the week is a healthy exercise that we need to practice until it becomes commonplace for us and our families.

I know a stay-at-home mom who dedicated more than twelve years to staying home with her three kids before slowly going back to work. In the years she was at home, her husband was working and traveling a lot, so she was often alone with the children. But she kept a 'tight ship' as it were. She ensured that the house was spotless and paid close attention to the children's education. She did the most amazing things with her kids, especially craft activities. She learned to treat her children with homeopathy. She even managed the build of her brand-new house and renovated another. When she thought they were big enough, she enrolled in a training program where she learned to help adult refugees and immigrants learn to write and read. After a couple of years teaching in a local NGO, she decided to open her own not-for-profit with three other women. To this day, her organization continues to focus on giving adults education to allow them to integrate into society. As one of the mothers I admire most in my life, she is the best example of a growth mindset.

I hope her example can inspire mothers that have decided to have a career break and focus on their family. Dr. Patricia Widmer, Director for Diversity and Management Programmes at the University of St. Gallen where she is responsible for the Women Back to Business Programme, told to me in an interview:

"During a break due to a prolonged maternity leave, a woman can learn new skills, maintain and increase her network, volunteer... don't just stop developing yourself and isolate yourself at home with your children. My advice is: if you decide to take a career break, for whatever reason, do it consciously and with a plan. Cultivating your ambitions and growth mindset while having a professional break will allow you to bounce forward quicker and better."

Ambition is a Mindset

How can cultivating a growth mindset help nourish people's ambitions and, ultimately, increase achievements and successes? In my opinion, the following are very important elements.

Lucidity to set clear and ambitious goals

–

The ability to overcome the fear of failure

All of the successful working mothers I have met had very clear professional aspirations. None of them told me "It happened by chance, and voila! Now I'm an accomplished woman." They all worked intensely toward their goals by using their **Ambition Factor** as a compass. They cultivated their growth mindset, and they were ready to 'bounce back' when they failed.

Thanks to all the fantastic women surrounding me and my own experiences, I have learned that working hard is not enough. We need to face challenges by embracing our fears, learn from failure, and stay positive and ambitious. And this is only possible if we have a growth mindset.

Ambition will separate our dreams from our goals: the **Ambition Factor** is what pushes us to work toward our success and towards accomplishing the goals we set. Without **Ambition Factor**, our dreams will remain dreams.

**The Ambition Factor
is what pushes us to
work toward our
success and toward
accomplishing
the goals we set.**

Who is Valeria? I am Valeria. You are Valeria. She is your best friend, your confidant, your coworker. She could be the owner of the flower shop around the corner, or the accountant in your company. She could be the next leader, the next multi-millionaire entrepreneur, or the next bestselling author.

She represents any mother around the world who is facing the daily challenges of being an ambitious professional while cultivating a balanced lifestyle.

Like her, we face all kinds of doubts. We keep questioning our decisions. We lose focus on our objectives and prioritizations between family and work. Valeria shows us what can happen if we do not build an equal and balanced relationship with our life partner, or if we forget to take care of ourselves. And like her, we can ask for support, look deep into our motivations, reshape our lifestyle and keep thriving.

*We all remember the stories we read as a child, and as mothers, we are reading tales to our children. Every tale has its hero, its obstacle, its lesson-learned, and happy ending. Let's be Valeria! Let her inspire you to keep on track with your goals and well-being. Let her inspire you to be aware of your **Ambition Factor.***

The idea of this book was born in December 2019, and I started working on it with Birdhaus Writers in January 2020. My life and the world around me at that time were very different. The year 2020 will remain forever the year of COVID-19. The impact this pandemic had on the planet was immense and unexpected, and it will take years to recover from its consequences. In May 2020 I had the option to try to keep my business running while hoping for the best, or to reshape my plans while accepting the new reality of a world living with a virulent virus without a cure and vaccine. I chose the latter option, which pushed us to create a new phrase 'social distancing'. I decided to close my business and refocus my priorities. This book is my response to a challenging 2020.

Looking into the eyes of our new reality and reshaping my goals according to the new normal has been a necessary journey, but it's still not over. Talking with other ambitious working mothers, listening to their struggles and creative solutions reinforced my willingness to go deeper in researching what ambition means to us. To finish this book and shared wisdom with other women became my mission in 2020.

Like every complex project in life, the lessons have been immense. But one stands out significantly. I managed to conquer a new personal frontier: wake up early and dedicate the first hour of the day to my well-being and objectives (Thank you, Robin Sharma and The 5AM Club).

Ambition Factor aims to provide every woman with enough elements to start a self-reflection journey and analyze the relationship with their ambition. I would be delighted to receive your thoughts via email after you've read my book!

Write your story, embrace your Ambition Factor and live the life you are meant to live.

Acknowledgements

Writing Ambition Factor has been a long and difficult journey which was made possible only thanks to a tribe of women, and a few men.

How do I start this section when we know there are many people that require my thanks? If my first novel required a team to be published, this book has been finished thanks to a village of people. Let's go in chronological order.

Thank you to:

— Birdhaus Writers Group: Lisa, Francesca, Friederike, Cindia, Elodie, Ruzica, Sandra, Franzisca. We all manage to get to write our book!

— Francesca, the designer of Birdhaus Writers. She was with me from the beginning. With passion and diligence, she transformed my cover ideas, and this book layout into something unique.

— All the women I have interviewed for my blog and for this book. Some of their interviews are online, some not, but all of them have contributed immensely to this book. A special thank you to the working mothers Kamalesh, Amanda, Barbara, Patricia, Christina, Simona and Assem.

— LeanIn – Supermom circle in Zurich for giving me the chance to meet the mothers for the focus group.

— Sandra for being part of Birdhaus Writers and for contributing her nutrition advice to this book.

— Angela, who helped me go through the closure of my coworking space and find my path back to writing and thriving in life.

— Aurelie, who was the first to read a VERY raw manuscript, encouraged me to continue.

— Lyndsay, who transformed my manuscript into a book worthy of reading and helped me shape Valeria's story.

— Gareth from Authoright for helping me with the publishing process and patiently waited for my manuscript (which arrived after a four-month delay).

— Mara, Nadine and Julia, Birdhaus Advisors and friends, for supporting me during the difficult time when Birdhaus closed. This book started in a moment of business growth, was written in a moment of business low, and was published in a moment of business development. They were here for me all along the journey.

— Leela, my web designer who makes magic with my ideas and helped me create the website and the questionnaire.

— Lucas and Lucas Design team for the consultancy on the book and website design.

A special thank you to Heather McGregor and Tiffany Dufu. Even if I never met them and only interacted with them via social media, I feel like both are my career mentors and life coaches. Their contribution to the world with their works and book is invaluable. They changed the way I think and behave for the better and are the leading inspiration for this book.

Thank you also to Masterclass and its writers' classes. Two writers helped me tremendously with this book: Neil Gaiman provided me with the inspiration to create Valeria story out of Cinderella, and Malcolm Gladwell made me understand we can also create good narrative within nonfiction books.

And of course, thank you to my husband, Riccardo. Nothing is possible without his unconditional love and support.

Endnotes

1 Mcgregor, Heather (2013) *'Mrs Moneypenny's Career Advice for Ambitious Women'*, Portfolio Publishing

2 *Cambridge Dictionary* (2020) Cambridge University Press, [Retrieved from https://dictionary.cambridge.org/dictionary/english/ambition] visited in January 2021.

3 Schank, Hana and Wallace, Elizabeth (2018) *'The Ambition Decisions: What Women Know About Work, Family, and the Path to Building a Life'*, Viking.

4 Ibid.

5 Vuleta, Christina (2017) *'The Ambition Gap: How Age And Economic Development Impact Women's Aspirations'*, Forbes Women, April 5, 2017, [Retrieved from https://www.forbes.com/sites/christinavuleta/2017/04/05/the-ambition-gap-how-age-and-economic-development-impact-womens-aspirations/] visited in January 2021.

6 Fels, Ana (2004) *'Necessary Dreams: Ambition in Women's Changing Lives'*, Anchor Publishing.

7 Fels, Anna (2004b) *'Do Women Lack Ambition?'*, Harvard Business Review, April 2004 Issue. [Retrieved from www.HBR.com] visited in January 2021.

8 Ibid.

9 Ibid.

10 Ibid.

11 Abouzahr, Katie, et al. (2017) *'Dispelling the Myths of the Gender: The Ambition Gap'*, Boston Consulting Group.

12 Scarpaleggia, Simona (2019) *'The Other Half: Creating Gender-Balanced Teams for Sustainability'*, LID Publishing.

13 Key performance indicators

14 Scarpaleggia, op. cit.

15 Lagarde, Christine and Solberg, Erna (2018) *'Why 2018 Must be the Year for Women to Thrive'*, We Forum, [Retrieved from https://www.weforum.org/agenda/2018/01/the-time-has-come-for-women-to-thrive-heres-how/] visited in January 2021.

16 Scarpaleggia, op. cit.

[17] Gonzales, Christian, et al. (2015) *'Fair Play: More Equal Laws Boost Female Labor Force Participation', The International Monetary Fund,* February 23, 2015 [Retrieved from https://www.imf.org/en/Publications/Staff-Discussion-Notes/Issues/2016/12/31/Fair-Play-More-Equal-Laws-Boost-Female-Labor-Force-Participation-42721].

[18] Ibid.

[19] Lagarde and Solberg, op. cit.

[20] Gonzales, op. cit.

[21] Fels (2004b), op. cit.

[22] McGregor, op. cit.

[23] Dotti, Sani, et al. (2016) *'Educational Gradients in Parents' Childcare Time Across Countries', Journal of Marriage and Family,* 1965–2012.

[24] Bühlmann, Felix, et al. (2009) *'The division of labour among European couples: The effects of life course and welfare policy on value–practice configurations', European Sociological Review,* 26(1): 49–66.

[25] Ibid.

[26] Ibid.

[27] Giudici, Francesco and Schumacher, Reto. (2017) *'The work of mothers in Switzerland: evolution and individual determinants', Social Change in Switzerland,* 10: doi: 10.22019/SC-2017-00005.

[28] Ibid.

[29] *'Advance and HSG Gender Intelligence Report (2020) Accerlerating Diversity with the Gender Maturity Compass 2020', Advance Gender Equality in Business,* [Retrieved from https://advance-hsg report.ch/uploads/media/default/45/Gender%20 Intelligence%20Report%202020%20Online%20PDF.pdf] visited in January 2021.

[30] Fuchs, Reiner and Lardi, Kamales (2013) *'Social Media Strategy, A Step by Step Guide for Building Your Social Business', Vdf Hochschulverlag an der ETH Zürich,* 1st edition Word Wise: Enabled.

[31] Rosling-Ronnlund, Anna, et al. (2018) *'Factfulness: Ten Reasons We're Wrong About the World—And Why Things Are Better Than You Think',* Flatrion Books.

[32] Abouzahr, op. cit.

33 Orme-Johnson, David W. and Barnes, Vernon A. (2014) *'Effects of the transcendental meditation technique on trait anxiety: a meta-analysis of randomized controlled trials'*, J Altern Complement Med. 20(5): 330–41.

34 Bonus, Katherine, et al. (2003) *'Alterations in Brain and Immune Function Produced by Mindfulness Meditation'*, Psychosomatic Medicine, 65(4): 564–70.

35 *'Why Lack of Sleep is Bad for Your Health'* (2018) National Health Service, [Retrieved from: https://www.nhs.uk/live-well/sleep-and-tiredness/why-lack-of-sleep-is-bad-for-your-health/)] visited in January 2021.

36 Sullivan, Kelly L (2017) *'Men with Children Sleep Fine; Women Not So Much'*, MedPage Today, AAN February 27, 2017. [Retrieved from: https://digitalcommons.georgiasouthern.edu/pubhlth-bee-facmedia/17/] visited in January 2021.

37 Doheny, Kathleen (2017) *'Moms Get Less Sleep than Dads'* Chicago Tribute, [Retrieved from https://www.chicagotribune.com/lifestyles/health/sc-moms-get-less-sleep-than-dads-health-0308-20170228-story.html] visited in January 2021.

38 Frappier, Julie, et al. (2013) *'Energy Expenditure during Sexual Activity in Young Healthy Couples'*, PLoS One 8(10): e79342.

39 Brody, Stuart (2010) *'The Relative Health Benefits of Different Sexual Activities'*, Journal of Sexual Medicine, Apr;7(4 Pt 1):1336-61. doi: 10.1111/j.1743-6109.2009.01677.x

40 Debrot, Anik, et al. (2017) *'More than just sex: Affection mediates the association between sexual activity and well-being'* Pers Soc Psychol Bull 43(3):287–99.

41 Rogers, Pamela (2018) *'The Health Benefits of Sex'*, healthline.com [Retrieved from https://www.healthline.com/health/healthy-sex-health-benefits] visited in January 2021.

42 Loewenstein, George and Krishnamurti, Tamar (2015) *'Does Increased Sexual Frequency Enhance Happiness?'* Journal of Economic Behavior & Organization 116(C):206–18.

43 Schank and Wallace, op. cit.

44 Wittenberg-Cox, Avivah, (2017) *'If You Can't Find a Spouse who Can't support Your Career, Stay Single'* Harvard Business Review, October 2017 [Retrieved from: https://hbr.org/2017/10/if-you-cant-find-a-spouse-who-supports-your-career-stay-single] visited in January 2021.

45 Sandberg, Sheryl (2013) *'Lean In: Women Work and the Will to Lead'*, Knopf Doubleday.

[46] Dufu, Tiffany, (2018) *'Drop the Ball: Achieving More by Doing Less'*, Flatiron Books.

[47] Ibid.

[48] Vanderkam, Laura (2015) *'I Know How She Does It: How Successful Women Make the Most of their Time'*, Penguin.

[49] Williams, Joan C (2004) *'The Maternal Wall'*, Harvard Business Review [Retrieved from https://hbr.org/2004/10/the-maternal-wall] visited in January 2021.

[50] Aristotle. *Politics: Book One* 1.1253a.

[51] Grant, Adam and Sandberg, Sheryl (2017) *'Option B: Facing Adversity, Building Resilience and Finding Joy'*, Knopf Doubleday.

[52] Casnocha, Ben and Hoffman, Reid (2012) *'The Start-Up of You: Adapt to the Future, Invest in Yourself, and Transform your Career'*, Currency.

[53] *'Facing the Job Crisis'* (2019) *Organization for Economic Co-Operation and Development*, [Retrieved from http://www.oecd.org/employment-outlook/2020/)] visited in January 2021

[54] *Collins Dictionary* (1979) [Retrieved from www.collins.co.uk] visited in January 2021

[55] Gilovich, Thomas and Medvec-Husted, Victoria (1995) *'The Experience of Regret: What, When, and Why'*, Psychological Review 102(2):379–95.

[56] Lamb, Amanda (2007) *'Smotherhood: Wickedly Funny Confessions from the Early Years Skirt!'*

[57] Tediosi, Ana Paula (2019) *'Meet Another Working Mom: interview with Amanda Lambe'* [Retrieved from http://anajustana.com/meet-another-working-mom-amanda-lambe/)]

[58] Tediosi Ana Paula, (2018) *'Next 9'*, Amazon Direct Publishing.

[59] Harvey, Mara (2018) *'Women and Risk'*, Nicolai Publishing & Intelligence GmbH.

[60] Dweck, Carol S (2008) *'Mindset: The New Psychology of Success'*, Ballantine Books.

[61] Vanderkam, Laura (2016) *'How to Gain Control of Your Free Time'* TedX Talk [Retrived from: https://www.ted.com/talks/laura_vanderkam_how_to_gain_control_of_your_free_time?language=en] visited in January 2021

www.ingramcontent.com/pod-product-compliance
Lightning Source LLC
LaVergne TN
LVHW051411080426
835508LV00022B/3033